LEARN Python

From Kids & Beginners

Up to Expert Coding

Dominique ♦ SAGE

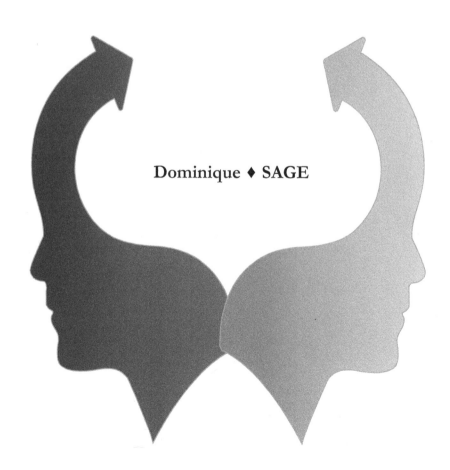

Table of Contents

BOOK #1: KIDS & BEGINNERS

BOOK #2: UP to EXPERT CODING

BOOK #1: KIDS & BEGINNERS

LEARN Python
From Kids & Beginners

Dominique ♦ SAGE

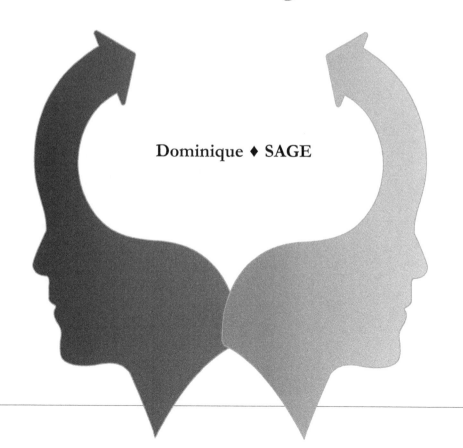

Introduction

"You're braver than you believe, and stronger than you seem, and smarter than you think." - A. A. Milne

Programming has become an invaluable skill even to those who aren't interested in software development and that is probably one of the reasons why you are here. If you're looking for a hands-on guide to teach you the ropes about Python programming and programming in general, then this book seeks to offer you a helping hand.

As someone with a computer science degree, but who also started very late in life learning how to code, I want to teach you as early as possible. I always wished my parents pushed me to learn programming from a young age, but I had to go to college to discover this new love. I want to share this love of programming with you and show you that it is not rocket science, despite what some believe.

Programming is no different from reading and writing. All it takes is practice, and a guiding hand to help you through the frustrating parts. In this book you will be guided through the fundamental concepts behind Python programming and you will learn step by step everything from installing Python to developing games.

You will start by preparing your work environment and acquiring every tool you need. Then you will study what variables are, how functions are created, and why loops and conditional statements can make programs to be so intelligent.

I have spent nearly 20 years in the industry programming applications, games, as well as personal projects. With this book, I want to dedicate my time to sharing my expertise and experience with those who dream to one day become programmers, game developers, software developers, or those who just want to learn what all the fuss is about. So let's get started!

Chapter 1:

Getting Started

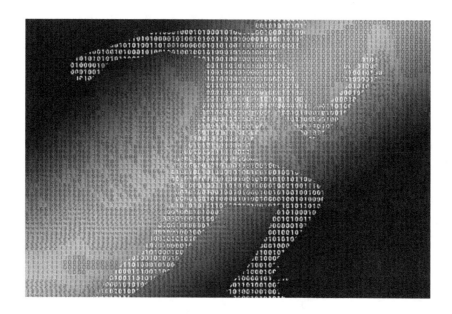

In this day and age, programming has become nearly as essential as learning how to read and write. It is a valuable skill that anyone can use, even if they aren't programmers. For instance, a boring task like sending emails with news updates and company business updates can easily be automated through the power of coding. There is no need to perform boring tasks manually when a simple program can be written to do the work for you. This is why learning how to program is so important. It can help anyone no matter where they are in life.

The good news is, learning how to program isn't even as difficult as many like to believe. Everyone can learn how to program in any language. That's right, no matter your age and your schooling, you can learn how to code. Children don't need to be "talented", or have some special skills in mathematics in order to get started. The entire world is being digitized and automated. Not learning how to code in the next decade will most likely leave a young person with a serious disadvantage in life, but fortunately, it is really simple to get started.

Learning how to program has never been easier. Nowadays, every company and organization requires some level of programming or interaction with technology. But programming isn't just a useful tool, it is also fun! Coding is all about the ability to solve problems. It is about researching, brainstorming, and fitting the puzzle pieces together. It can even be about art and creativity. Many programmers, myself included, have built a passion for programming due to the ability to create fun games! Your child can easily learn to direct his or her creativity into creating a whole new world, with a story, and interesting scenarios. Many programmers choose the artistic route because they need to explore their creativity.

But what about applications? Aren't they far more complex? The answer is no! Mobile apps, games, fancy software, they all rely on the same concepts we are going to explore in this book. It is easy to encourage your child to have fun with technology and create something, because all it takes is understanding the building blocks well enough to place them in a certain order, often creative.

In addition to all of the aforementioned benefits, programming is often a group activity. Whether creating applications or games, your child will have the chance to interact and socialize with other like minded children. There are many online groups, programming clubs, online academies, and other social channels where your child will be able to learn with others how to solve problems, create something out of nothing, and above all make some new friends.

With that being said, in this chapter we are going to start our journey by learning all the basics. So let's get started and explore the wonderful world of programming by first learning the basics.

The Basics

Nowadays, everything is computerized, whether it's a phone, watch, vacuum cleaner, doorbell, you name it. We use programming to tell all of those gadgets what to do. Keep in mind that this also includes applications. We tell them what to do and they do it. For instance, we can create a simple game, which is also an application that will let us take control of a spaceship model, move it up and down and fire rockets. These applications can take anywhere from a few lines of codes to thousands. This might sound scary at first, but the idea is to solve one tiny problem at a time. You don't look at a book and think it's too long and scary to even bother reading it, right? Of course not! You go chapter by chapter, page by page and absorb its knowledge.

So how do we start? Where do we even begin? Using our spaceship example, we would begin by drawing or writing down our idea. The best approach is to lay down our thoughts on a piece of paper. We can use our imagination and think about what we need to do and what problem needs to be solved. Once we have a plan, we can start coding. But to do all that, first we need to download and install certain tools that will allow us to program an application or game. In this chapter, we are going to focus on preparation. After all, before you can write your homework you need some paper and a pen. Our programming tools are no different than just that.

In order to start programming, we need to understand the computer's language. Computers don't speak like us. They take commands, one at a time, and unfortunately they don't speak plain English, so we need to learn the computer's language. Programming is done in a number of languages that any computer can understand, such as C, C++, Python, JavaScript, Ruby, and many more. All of these languages enable us to instruct our computer what to do. In this book, however, we are going to explore Python, which is a simple language, but powerful enough to let you code pretty much everything, including games.

Python is a fully-featured programming language that is taught in many courses around the world. Some start learning it in elementary school, while others study it in software engineering and computer science classes at university. This powerful, yet easy to understand programming language, is even used by some of the most popular technologies in the world. For instance, YouTube and Gmail are some of the most famous examples, among many more. Now, to get you on your path to learning Python, we need to perform three actions. We first need to download Python from the official website, and then install it on your computer.

Once you have done that, we can give it a try by creating a basic program. But first, why learn Python at all? If you like games or if you look at the big software developers, you will see that many of them use C++, C#, or other languages.

Why Python is the Best Starting Point?

Python is a programming language that is recommended to children and beginners in particular for one simple reason. It is the most easy to read and understand language out there because of its similarity to written English. While other languages may have some unordinary keywords or a seemingly strange syntax, Python is as close to English as it gets. Here's a simple example using the traditional first program that every beginner writes when barely starting out:

print ("Hello, world!")

As you can see, you don't need any programming knowledge to understand what's going on. It's so simple even a child can understand this line without knowing anything about coding. We'll talk more about what's happening in this simple program later. For now, you and your child should know that Python is much easier to read and write than other more sophisticated programming languages. This example, although extremely rudimentary, is no different from the more complex programs written in Python. They will simply be collections of lines of code similar to the one above. With that being said, let's see the other reasons why your child should start out with Python instead of other languages and why you should encourage their interests early on:

1. Python is intuitive: We already talked about this briefly, but it can't be said often enough. Python reads like plain English. That is why even elementary schools and high schools are starting to implement Python programming into their curriculum. Python is the perfect language to get kids interested in coding because it allows them to turn their creative ideas into tangible results on the computer screen. They can imagine a program or a game and then simply write it using some basic logic. In addition, Python involves a lot less lines of code necessary to take a certain action. For instance, Java and C++, although industry standards and very popular programming languages, require a lot more steps to perform an action. That means that a child would have to struggle more to write down the same idea, and that can easily build up frustration. What we want is for the child to have fun while learning because that will drive him even more.

Python simply makes sense and it allows children to focus on learning how to think logically and how to solve problems, instead of fighting complex coding syntax.

2. Python is accessible: Another major advantage is the fact that Python is easy to install at home and it is freely available. Python doesn't require a license, therefore you don't need to pay anything to use it. It is available through an open source license, meaning that anyone can use it whether for education or even commercially. You are even allowed to write your own Python distributions and libraries and then sell them, even though they are still similar to the official release. Who knows, maybe your kid will hit it big, and it won't even cost him or her anything. While on the financial topic, you as a parent should also know that you don't need any kind of fancy tech to install Python. All you need is a desktop or laptop computer, and it doesn't matter what operating system it's running. Whether you have a machine that works with Windows, Linux, or Mac, you can install Python just as easily on all three. All you need to do is visit the official page, download Python and follow the installation process. We'll talk more about this in the next section.

3. Python helps with child development: Python, or programming in general, isn't only for those who are determined to pursue a career in computer science or game development. Programming can help a child develop problem solving skills that are so crucial in our daily lives. Furthermore, it helps them develop the ability to think critically. But the benefits don't stop there. Even if you think your child may not be interested in programming or mathematics later in life, learning how to program will help him or her to develop skills in writing and thinking creatively as well. It's all due to the fact that your child will have to combine critical thinking with creativity in order to solve problems when creating programs or games. This combination between logic and creativity will have a powerful impact no matter what the child will choose to do in later years.

4. Python is here to stay: Python has established itself as one of the best languages not just for beginners, but for industry experts as well. For instance, Python is also used in computer science, analytics, machine learning, artificial intelligence development, robotics and a lot more. It is a

powerful, versatile and efficient language that can be used with anything, and it can be later combined with other more complex programming languages like C++. Because of these points, Python is quite future proof, and even ten to twenty years from now your child may still be working with Python. As mentioned earlier, Python today is used behind some of the most powerful technologies and corporations in the world. Amazon, Google, Facebook, NASA, YouTube and many more rely on Python. Because the language is such a core element of all of these big names, it will not go away any time soon. And even if somehow Python would disappear into the void, it is so easy to transfer to another programming language when you have already mastered one. For instance, most people who are experts in Python can become proficient programmers in other languages like C# or JavaScript within weeks, not years.

If you are still not sure whether Python is the right starting point for your child, there are other alternatives. Perhaps your child is still too young, or you are worried that focusing on the language's syntax may prove to be too challenging and frustrating. That is not a problem! If you child is too young for a fully featured programming language, you might want to look into an alternative such as Scratch. Scratch is something known as a visual, block-based programming language developed by MIT and aimed purely at children with the purpose of introducing them to the world of programming. All the user needs to do is head to the official website, and use a block-like user interface to create any project.

This alternative cannot be called a proper programming language becomes it is not fully customizable by the programmer and it is limited when it comes to complex projects. However, it is aimed at children above the age of 8, and because of its visual focus your child can purely focus on developing his or her creativity and problem solving skills without worrying about programming theory and coding syntax. The creators of Scratch have realized that the skills needed to code computer applications have become an important aspect of literacy. Therefore, this alternative to Python still pushes the child to design projects, solve problems, and share ideas with a vast online community.

In this book, however, we will focus on Python, but you should still look into Scratch as a simple online, readily available alternative if you think it would be better as a starting point. Once your child grows out of Scratch, Python will be there waiting to stimulate his or her creativity and way of thinking even more.

Now, let's get back to Python and start installing it on your computer.

Installing Python

As mentioned earlier, Python is free and we can download it from the official website at https://www.python.org/. To download Python, all you need to do is go over the download menu and navigate to the correct operating system section. If your computer runs on Windows, simply click on Windows and then select the latest version of Python to download.

Below are the steps for Windows computers:

1.   Click on "Downloads".

2.   Click on "Windows".

3.   Click on the latest version of "Python"

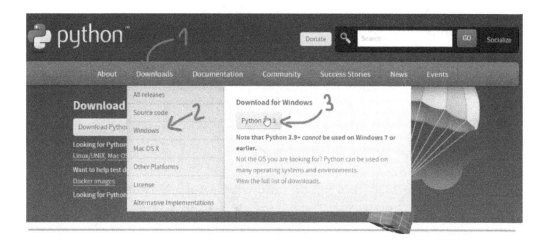

Do the same if your machine runs on Mac OS X, Linux, or any other type of system. When the download is finished, you will most likely find it on your computer's "download" folder or directory. Simply double click on the downloaded file to begin the actual installation process.

When we install Python, we will also automatically install IDLE. This is a tool where we will type our code. It is similar to a word processor, like Microsoft Word or Google Docs, but it is used to write and edit code instead of simple text. The installation process is very simple and straightforward, so simply follow the instructions. As usual, you will have to click on "next" a few times, wait for the installation process to complete and done, Python is ready to go.

As an alternative to installing Python on your computer, you can also use the online interactive *shell*, found on the official Python website at https://www.python.org/shell/. In programming terms, a *shell* is simply a computer window that allows you to type lines of code or commands that the computer will execute. The online *shell* works nearly the same as the one provided through IDLE, except that you can't save your work. So, if you want to quickly do some exercises while learning, you can just launch the online *shell* and play around. This is a great alternative if you or your child travel a lot, or need to switch systems fairly often. Python can always be at your fingertips.

Your First Program

Now, let's run IDLE and try it out. Go to your start menu, or wherever you chose to install Python and IDLE and then run it. You will see that IDLE is also a text-based user interface like the online *shell* and you will use it to type in lines of Python commands. When you first open the window, the first thing you will see is this symbol ">>>". This is the command prompt and it symbolizes that the program, or system, is ready to take in your instructions. In other words, we can start programming! So let's type the following line:

print ("Hello, world!")

Now, hit the Enter or Return button on the keyboard and observe how the *shell* will answer to you. You will see that a line of text, namely "Hello, world!", will be printed to your screen. Congratulations, you just wrote your first program! Yes, it is indeed a program, and it is the first one all programmers write when they start out. Why is it a program, you ask? Well, our goal was to have a certain line of text displayed on the screen for us. We have written a line of code that solved our problem and achieved our goal. In other words, we have built an application, no matter how basic it is. Now let's take a side step and see what happens in our little program.

Lines of code are broken down into basic elements, or building blocks. Thinking of playing with Legos and thinking how to combine each block to create something fun and exciting. Programming in general follows the same principle. Our program starts with the keyword "print". This is called a function and functions are the ones that command the computer to do something for us. The reason we know that this is a function is because it is followed by parentheses that contain some information. Inside the parentheses we typed an output that we want the function to display. Print is a simple example of one of the many functions that are found by default in Python. They are also known as built-in functions, which means that we can always use them in any program we write. We can also create our own custom functions, but we won't discuss that right now.

Inside the parentheses, we have a short sentence, "Hello, world!". In programming, this sentence would also be called a sequence of characters, and they are enclosed in quotation marks. The quotation marks are important, because anything outside of them is a direct command to the computer. Inside the quotation marks we have something that is called a string. This means, that "Hello, world!" is not a command the computer needs to execute. It is just a piece of text that means nothing to the computer. It's just something we want to be displayed on our screens, as a message.

Normally, programs will be longer than this one, but the *shell* we're using at the moment isn't the best option. In this case we need to use a code editor instead. Fortunately, Python already comes with an editor option and all we need to do in IDLE is click on File to open the menu and then select File > New File. This will launch a new window, labeled as "untitled".

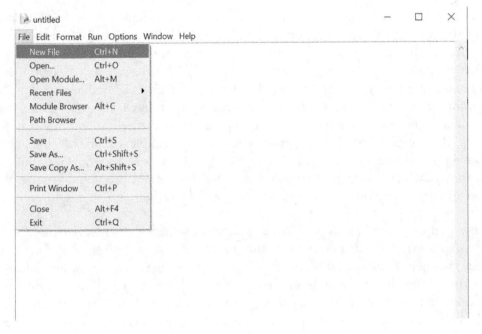

Let's start writing a slightly more complex program. Type the following lines in the editor:

```
# MyProgram.py

myName = input ("What's your name?\n")

print ("Hello, ", myName)
```

The very first line we have is not an actual command or line of code. It is called a comment and we can identify it because the line starts with the hash symbol "#". Everything after a hash symbol is ignored by the program and the computer doesn't do anything. The purpose of these comments is to remind us as programmers what the purpose of our code block is. Writing informative comments will also help other programmers that might be working with us in understanding how our code works. Imagine starting to write a game and you decide to take a break and work on something else. When you come back to that game, you will probably be confused and you will have to read and reread your code, figuring out line by line what you wanted to do. However, with the help of comments, you or your friends will know immediately what the idea behind the code was.

In the second line of the program we simply ask the program's user to write down his name. Once he declares his name, the program will remember it in the form of the variable we created, called "myName". By creating this variable, we will be able to call it in the next line. The third line simply prints "Hello, " and the name of the user that was memorized by the program earlier. You will also notice that we left a space after the comma, and before closing the quotes. That's because empty spaces between words need to be specified, otherwise the computer won't know how to separate words from each other.

Now we can execute our new program by clicking on the Run menu and choosing "Run Module".

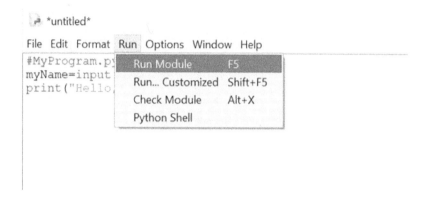

 At this point, the editor will ask you to save your program first. Remember that it is still called "untitled" by default. We are going to name it "MyProgram" as mentioned in our first line comment. The computer will now save the application under the file name "MyProgram.py". As you might've guessed, "py" is short for Python. Now that the program is saved, it will start running. The Python *shell* will open and the program will display the question "What's your name?". All you need to do is answer what your program wants, for instance with "Bob", and it will print out "Hell, Bob". Now, since this is all we told our program to do, it will immediately shut down after printing the message and you will see the editor prompt once again, to write more code.

Programs take things literally. In a way they are like little children. You say "eat your vegetables" and sometimes they will do as you say, like a kid. But most of the time, they will give you an error, like a smarty pants, and just wait staring at you because you forgot to give the instructions to pick up the fork and stick it into the vegetable. This is why programming is sometimes relaxing (or frustrating) to adults, but amusing to children. You need to spell it all out and be creative.

Now take a short break with your child and get creative! That's right, you already have enough information to start playing around with the program. Your young coder will certainly like how the computer seems to speak to him. It's like watching a cartoon where the computer speaks and interacts directly with the character. So let your child have some fun. Add more lines to the code that ask for age or hobbies. Let your child spell out his or her name multiple times. Kids amuse themselves making the computer spell out their name a dozen times in a row. Above all, make learning a fun experience and soon you will see that learning how to program turns into playing with the computer.

Summary

Python programming and programming in general is nothing but a game about solving puzzles and finding creative solutions. Everything starts out with a problem. After all, an application is a solution to a problem we're all having. You use everything you know about programming to solve that problem and in the process you will learn something new. Problem solving also involves research, so it's impossible to not add to your treasure trove of knowledge. At the end of the day, you trained your brain like a muscle and you feel happy for finding the answer to your riddle.

In this chapter, we have solved more than just one problem. We learned why Python is the perfect start, we have successfully installed it on our systems and we even started coding, with very little knowledge. It's like learning how to speak a new language isn't it? As soon as you learn 10 words, you start mixing them to see what sentences you can make. Same thing with coding. In the next chapter, you will add to your known words and learn how to solve even more problems. So keep your Python editor handy and let's have some fun!

Chapter 2:

Fun with Variables

So far we only wrote a couple of basic programs that don't really do all that much. The first just displays a plain message, and the second one is quite plain even though we can interact with it and even expand it a little. In this chapter we are going to dig a little deeper to get a better understanding about programming and learn how to make more intelligent programs.

In the previous chapter we also mentioned something called a variable. In this chapter we will study a little bit of theory because a solid foundation is needed. It might be a tad boring, but we will mix it up with some fun examples. In this chapter we will learn what variables are, and we will explore the main categories of variables, namely numbers, strings, lists and more.

What's a Variable?

In our short problem we have created a variable called "myName", but what is it exactly? Variables are things which your computer will remember throughout the program. They contain certain information that we add to them. It's like adding some songs to your phone. The phone remembers them until you delete them, and you can always listen to them. Variables work in the same way, but it stores the information you add to the variable in the computer's own memory. The purpose of variables is to have an easier way to access a bunch of information.

For instance, in our previous program we could also use the variable's information without needing the variable itself. However, if we would need that information more than once in our program, we would have to rewrite the same line of code multiple times. By creating a variable and writing the information into it, all we need to do is call onto that variable. Writing one word several times throughout your program is easier than writing several lines of code every time you need them.

Variables come in different types and Python can remember them all. For instance, we can have numbers like 42 and 23.99. But, we can also have strings, which include words, letters, and anything that you can type with the help of your keyboard.

In most programming languages, Python included, we need to assign a value to a variable. We do this by using the equal sign. For example, "n = 10" means that we have assigned the value "10" to variable "n". So the computer will remember the value of 10, and we will have access to it whenever we call "n" to come out and play. We used the same process in our last program by assigning a string to a variable. Here's another example:

myName = "Max"

Remember that words are strings and that they need to be placed between quotation marks, otherwise we will get an error. In this example we assign the value of Max to the "myName" variable. As you can see, the rule is to declare the variable by writing its name first, and then use the "=" sign to declare its value on the right side.

Keep in mind that variables can have any name we want. In this example we have used "myName" because it describes the purpose and the content of the variable. We can also name it "my_awesome_and_amazing_name" though that might be a bit too long. It will still work just as fine. Variables can have any name we want, but it's easier to read them if they are related to whatever information they contain. However, there are some rules that we need to follow when naming the variable:

1.   The variable needs to start with a letter.

2.   Everything after the first letter can be other letters, or numbers and symbols. For example, we can also use the underscore symbol like so, my_name, and it will have the same

effect. You can write the names of your variables however you find them easier to read.

3.   We can't leave blank spaces. For example, if we would write "my name" instead of "myName" or "my_Name", we would get an error. Using a blank space to separate the words would cause Python to think that we are trying to declare two variables. But, since we're doing it wrong, we get an error.

4.   Python variables are case sensitive. What this means is that it matters whether we use lower case letters or we capitalize them. For instance, the variable myName is entirely different from the variable MyName. You can use both of them at the same time, but they will represent different values. It doesn't really matter whether you capitalize the first letter or not. You are free to choose. But, once you decide to go with a lowercase letter, you should use the same naming style throughout the program. This way we avoid any confusions. In this book, we are going to stick to naming our variables like this: myName, bigNumber, greenCar, and so on.

Now let's write another little program so we try out some variables and understand how they work. Create a new program and call it whatever you want, then type the following lines of code and save it:

```
myName = "Max"

myAge = 14

yourName = input ("What's your name?")

yourGame = input (" What's your favorite game?")

print ("My name is", myName, ", and I am", myAge, "years old")

print ("Your name is", yourName, ", and your favorite game is", yourGame)

print ("Let's play together")
```

This program is no different than the previous one we wrote. It just has more variables and more lines of code. We first instruct the program to memorize "myName" and "myAge". Then, whoever runs the application will be asked to introduce themselves by typing his or her name and favorite game. These values will then be memorized by the computer in the form of two other variables called "yourName" and "yourGame". We have an input function (more on functions later), which means that we want whoever is running the program to type something on their keyboard. This is also called "to input", which is the reason why the function is called an input. Finally, we have a bunch of strings written between quotation marks. These quotes are also called prompts because they prompt (ask) the user about the input. Finally, at the end of the program we command the program to print the values that are memorized by the variables. If you run the program correctly, you will see that the computer will remember everything you programmed it to remember.

Now that you have a rough understanding about variables and you know what they are and how they work, let's start talking about a particular type of variable: the number.

Numbers

As mentioned earlier, variables can be used as many times as we want in the same application without having to repeat the same code when we wrote it. One of these variables is all about numbers. After all, computers are great at doing math. In fact, computers can perform such difficult calculations in such a short time that no matter how good you are at math, you just can't compete. We may be better than computers at certain things, but mathematical processing isn't one of them. Fortunately, Python allows us to do a number of operations using four types of numbers, but in this section we will only focus on two of them because they are used in nine out of ten situations.

In Python we will be working with two categories of numbers, namely integers and floating point numbers. Integers are whole numbers only, such as 8, 453, 34, 0, -22, and so on. Keep in mind that zero is also an integer, as well as negative numbers as long as they are whole numbers. Floating numbers, on the other hand, are decimal numbers, like 2.1, 3.0, 0.256, and so on. The other two number types we have are Booleans and complex numbers. Booleans can be only two values, true or false. Simple as that! Complex numbers, on the other hand, involve complex mathematics, like working with imaginary numbers, so we won't be focusing on that, as fun as it sounds.

Integers are the most often used number type because whole numbers are used whenever you need to count something or when you're performing some basic math operations, like 10 - 2 = 8. For example, when you write a program that involves asking the user about his or her age, you will be using whole numbers, or integers in other words. After all, you won't say to anyone that you are 12.4 years old, right?

On the other hand, floating point numbers, or floats for short, are used when we need to work with fractions. For instance, when we need to find out the distance, or the weight of something, or prices and so on, we will use floats. For example, we will have a floating point number when we declare the price of a variable called "pizza":

pizzaPrice = 19.34

As you can see, we only used the number. Remember that when we use numbers, we can't add various symbols like the dollar sign, or pounds and so on.

With all that being said, numbers are mostly used to perform some kind of mathematical operations. But to perform those operations, we need to discuss operators.

Operators

In programming, as well as math, operators are symbols such as plus and minus. They are called this way because they are used to perform an operation, or a calculation on a series of numbers. For example, we perform such operations when using a simple pocket calculator (you kids still use those right?). You type 2 + 2 to perform an addition and learn the total sum of those two numbers. The plus sign in that simple calculation is the operator.

Python includes other operators as well, and some of them may differ from the ones you learned in school. The plus and minus operators, for instance, are the same, and they are represented by the + and - symbols. Division, however, is written using a forward slash, like so "/". Multiplication is also different. You probably learned to use "x" as the multiplication operator, like 2 x 2 = 4. However, in programming we use the asterisk symbol instead, like so: 2 * 2 = 4.

There are other operators as well, like exponents, but we are going to focus on the basics here. So let's continue to the next section and have fun with math!

Basic Python Math

Now that you know how numbers and operators work, we can start using Python as a calculator. In this section we only need the Python *shell* instead of the editor, so start it up like we did in chapter 1, or run the interactive online Python *shell* instead *(https://www.python.org/shell/)*. We don't need all the programming capabilities here because we won't create any fancy program, All we're going to do is play around with numbers and do some basic math. In case you don't remember because there's so much new knowledge to absorb, the *shell* is just a command line interface when you type commands for the computer to immediately execute. You will see the result instantly instead of writing a whole program, saving it and then running it to see the result.

Try out what we discussed by typing something like:

>>> 10 + 10

You will see that the Python *shell* will give you the answer immediately, which is 20. Start playing around with math this way. Do a number of calculations and see how Python can work exactly like a calculator.

Syntax Errors

While we're playing around with the Python *shell* we should discuss a little problem you may have already encountered, the problem of syntax errors. While experimenting with what you've learned so far, you probably typed a few lines of code that Python doesn't fully understand and what you got was an error. Whenever you type something that the programming language can't read, it will give you what's known as a syntax error. What this means is that you did not follow the programming rules of Python when writing your code.

Syntax is simply a collection of rules that you must follow or your code will not work as intended. These mistakes are syntax errors, and they are similar to making grammar mistakes on your English tests. Except that if someone reads your sentence, even though it has mistakes in it, that person will still understand it. Computers don't work like that. They are strict and they follow the rules. If you don't follow the same rules, they simply won't understand what you want them to do. Here's an example of how to get a syntax error:

10 + 10 equals?

The result will look something like this:

SyntaxError: invalid syntax

In this example we have mixed some plain English with the mathematical operation. The resulting error tells us that Python doesn't understand our command. If we replace this command by typing 10 + 10 instead, Python will perform the calculation correctly. Computers are dependable as long as we all speak the same language, in this case being Python, not English.

Using Variables

So far we used the *shell* by typing direct commands instead of declaring variables. As mentioned earlier, using the *shell* makes simple exercises easier because we don't need to create applications, write them, save them, run them and so on, just to get to the result. We can just run the Python *shell*, type a command or two and see what happens. We can do the same thing using variables like we did in the programs we wrote earlier. For instance, we can assign values to variables just like we did when we assigned the string "Max" to the "myName" variable.

By typing n = 10 in the *shell*, the value of 10 will be memorized as a value that belongs to the "n" variable. Whenever we invoke this variable in the *shell*, its value will be used. However, if we declare that n = 20 in the same command prompt, the new value "20" will be assigned to the variable instead. In a real program, this wouldn't work. We would get an error. Instead, we would have to scroll to the line where we declared the value of "n", and edit it in order to make the change. With that being said, let's type the following lines and see what happens:

n = 10

n

10

We assigned the value of 10 to the n variable, and in the next command prompt we involved the n variable. By invoking it, the *shell* printed its value, which is 10. Now let's type something else:

n = 20

n * 2

40

Notice that again we declared the variable in the same *shell*. This changed its value to 20. In the next line we performed a multiplication operation, but instead of using the value directly, we used the variable. Since the variable has a value of 20, multiplied by 2, the result 40 is printed. Now let's see a somewhat different example:

n = 10

n = n - 1

n

9

As you can see, we have our "n" variable both on the left and the right side of the equal operator. In basic math class, you may have learned that this isn't right, and in that case it's true. The statement isn't valid. However, in programming, it is entirely correct to write such a statement. Why? The computer looks at the right side of the operator first and performs the mathematical calculation. Once the result is obtained, it becomes the new value that is assigned to the variable. We declared that the value of n is 10, but by redeclaring it in the next line that the value is n - 1, which translated to 10 - 1, the new value of 9 is assigned.

Before continuing, let's perform one more operation using the division operator and see what happens:

n = 10

n / 2

5.0

As you can see, we wrote 10 divided by 2, which is equal to 5. But Python gave us 5.0 as a result, instead of just 5. This is because Python works with something that is called true division. Python gives us a floating point number as the result of a division simply because the result is more accurate and less likely to contain any errors. Other programming languages, however, will give us 5 as the result. It is not a big difference, just something to be aware of.

Strings

You will work a lot with numbers when programming, but what will you do when you need to write an application that interacts with people? After all, maybe you want to create a game and for that you need to allow players to "speak" to the game. This is where the strings we mentioned earlier come in.

People talk to each other using words and sentences. Computers like to speak in numbers, so if we want to make a program to talk to people, we need to use strings instead of numbers. We discussed earlier that strings are collections of characters. Basically anything that you type on your keyboard can form a string, whether it's letters, numbers or symbols. The biggest difference between number variables and strings though, is the fact that they are not used to calculate anything. Strings are just information that is sent to the user. So far we used strings together with the print function because this is the most popular way of using them. For instance, if you ask the user to input his name, the computer could print it afterwards in the form of a string. If you remember, we actually did that already. However, there's so much more we could do.

Let's change up a bit the program we created earlier. Let's ask the user for his name, but this time we are going to declare a variable which will contain his name. Then the program is going to print that name multiple times. To do that, we are going to use a technique you didn't learn yet called looping. We are going to use a loop to repeat the printing operation as many times as we want. We will talk more about loops in a later chapter, for now let's focus our attention on variables and strings. Let's write the following code:

Write the following code and run it (via the Run>Run Module menu):

Request the name of the user

userName = input ("What's your name?")

Print the user's name 99 times

for x in range (99):

      print (userName, end = " ")

In addition to the loop that was mentioned, we also have a new argument inside our print statement. In this example, we have added the "end" argument and it is equal to an empty space. Notice how in-between the quotation marks we left an empty space, like we leave normally between words in sentences. The space is still a string, even though you might say that there's nothing there. What the "end" argument actually means by having this string as a value, is that all print statements have to end with a space. You can change this argument to anything you want, and every loop that prints the statement will have that argument as a bonus added to it. For instance, you can replace the space with " is awesome at coding! "and the print will look something like "Max is awesome at coding!".

What you need to remember from this is that arguments are useful because they can add new options and conditions to a certain function, like in this case the print () function. This way we add a bit more detail to the function, making it more complex. In all programming languages adding arguments to functions is quite common, so take some time to play around with the ones you know, in this case the "end" argument. Just make sure to place the argument inside the parentheses after declaring the function, in this case print, and if you don't want an argument, you can leave the parentheses empty.

Lists

The beauty about variables is that they can be anything you want. So far they have been numbers, whether floating point numbers or integers, and strings, but they can also be lists. Lists are groups of items, like a shopping list. Each list item contains a value and they are all separated from each other using commas. In order to write a list, however, we need to use square brackets and place all of our items inside it. Lists are versatile and you can put anything you want in them. You can insert any type of value. You can either have lists of strings, numbers, mixed variables, or even lists containing lists. With that being said, here's a simple list and how you should write it:

myList = [apple, flour, pear, sugar]

This is a list of variables. We can declare these variables and assign them any values we want. Then we can use them inside a list, like this one. As mentioned earlier we can also have a list of strings. Here's another example:

myColors = ["green", "yellow", "blue"]

As you can see, we respect the rules of writing strings, by placing our string elements inside quotation marks even when declaring a list.

Now, let's see an example because practice is always more fun than boring theory. In this demonstration, we will be using the Turtle package. We didn't use packages yet in our examples, or modules as they are also called. For now you should know that Python packages are extensions of the programming language. They contain more functions and various data types that the basic version of Python doesn't contain. By using packages we can work faster because we don't have to write our own functions, we can just import what we need into our project by importing the right module. Python comes with hundreds of packages and modules that extend its functionality, but in this example we only need one and it's called Turtle. In a future chapter we will focus more on this package in particular, but for now we only need one of its functions, namely "numinput()". We are going to create a list of colors and then our new program will ask the user to type how many faces an object should have. This function from the Turtle package allows us to type in that number. Let's start by opening a new window and creating a new program. Don't forget to save it.

```
import turtle

p = turtle.Pen()

turtle.bgcolor ("black")

myColors = ["green", "blue", "yellow", "purple", "pink", "white", "red", "white"]

objectFaces = int (turtle.numinput ("Total number of faces",

"How many faces from 1 to 8 would you like to have?", 3, 2, 7))
```

(Source: **https://docs.python.org/3/library/turtle.html** retrieved in March 2021)

Let's stop here for a moment and discuss what we have so far. The first thing we need to do when we want to use a package is import it and that is done using the "import" keyword, followed by the name of the package. That's it! Now we have all the functions that are part of the Turtle module. Next up, we prepare the graphics and create the list of colors we want to have as options. Finally, we make our program smart enough to ask the user how many faces he wants the object to have. He can choose between one and eight faces, but if he doesn't want to choose, we will have a default selection of four faces. Now all we have left to do is write the code that draws the object. Keep in mind that this object needs to have as many faces as the user wants. With that being said, let's take a look at the code:

```
for x in range (360):

    p.pencolor (myColors [x % objectFaces])

    p.forward ( x * 3 / objectFaces + x)

    p.left (360 / objectFaces + 1)
```

Below is the complete program to run:

```
import turtle
p=turtle.Pen()
turtle.bgcolor("black")
myColors=["green","blue","yellow","purple","pink","white","red","withe"]
objectFaces=int(turtle.numinput("Total number of faces","How many faces from 1 to 8 would you like to have?",3,2,7))
for x in range(360):
    p.pencolor(myColors[x%objectFaces])
    p.forward(x*3/objectFaces+x)
    p.left(360/objectFaces+1)
```

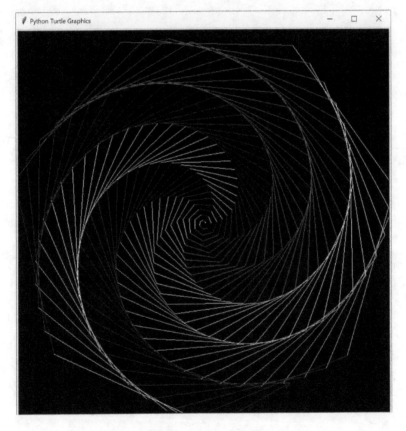

Above example when I ask for 7 faces :-)

As you can see, we are using a loop again to do the work for us. We will talk about loops in another chapter because they are important and you will be playing a lot with them. For now, let's talk about the three lines we wrote in the loop. In the first line, we tell the program to change the color of the Turtle pen so that it matches the number of colors to the number of faces the object has. This means that if the user declares four faces, we will have four colors to match each face. In the second line, we instruct the program to modify the length of the drawn line. The purpose of this command is to make sure that some objects don't appear smaller than others. We want shapes that are roughly the same size. In the third line of the "for" loop, we instruct the newly created object to rotate by a certain number of degrees. This number needs to be precise, so what we do in this line is divide 360 by how many sides the object has. This means that a circle that has one face will have an angle of 360 degrees. A square, on the other hand, will have four angles at 90 degrees, because 360 degrees is divided by four faces.

This program might be a little difficult to understand at first, but by playing with it you will learn in no time. After all, there's a lot going on in the few lines of code we have. We used a Python module for the first time, we used a list, and we did some math in order to draw the object and perform some operations. Play around with the code to understand it better. Don't be afraid of the math we used in it. If you don't fully understand it, change the values in the code and see what happens. By experimenting you will have fun obtaining weird, even ridiculous results, but you will also understand why we wrote the program the way we did. But most of all, have fun using your own creativity and see what happens.

Practical Python

So far you've learned quite a lot! You saw how Python works with various types of data, like strings, integers and lists, and you also played a bit with functions and loops. Python is a powerful programming language and its simplicity makes it fun. But, so far we have only talked about theory and written a few demonstrations to see that theory in action. Keep in mind that all of this is important and you can't advance in programming without learning that theory and how everything works. With that being said, your Python applications may have been somewhat fun so far, but they don't do much. So let's create our first program that will do something useful. In this section we are going to use the power of Python to create a calculator that does all the math for you. Say goodbye to worrying about your math homework!

To write this program we are going to use a combination of everything we talked about so far. However, a specific function is going to play a vital role, and that is the "eval" function. What this function will do in our calculator application is turn a question, or the user's input, such as "10 + 2" into an answer, or an output, such as 12 in this case. What this function does is evaluate your input, process it, and then reveal the solution to it. It will also allow us to display the problem and the answer at the same time on the screen, which makes our program a bit more useful than a typical calculator.

For this program, you will need to remember your mathematical operators. If you don't remember how to write all of them in Python, make sure to go back and refresh your memory. Don't forget that in Python you can't write 2 x 2, you need to write 2 * 2 instead to perform a multiplication. With that being said, let's take a look at our new program. Create a new Python file and save it.

```
print ("My_Awesome_Calculator.py")

mathProblem = input ("Type your math question, or 'E' to exit the program: ")

while (mathProblem != "E"):

        print ("The result to your", mathProblem, "is: ", eval (mathProblem))

        mathProblem = input ("Type another math question, or "E" to exit the
program:")
```

To summarize, the program will ask the user to type a problem or to type the letter "E" if he or she wants to quit the application. The program will keep executing until the user chooses to exit the program. Next, we use the eval function to display both the problem and the solution to it at the same time. Once an answer is given, the program will again ask for another question or for the user to quit if there are no other math problems to be solved. This is why we are using the "while" loop to create this calculator. Basically, while the user has problems to solve, the program will keep running as designed. When we hit the "E" letter on the keyboard, the program will stop running because there are no more problems, therefore the loop will also stop executing. This is the beauty of while loops. They will keep repeating until its condition is no longer met. In this case, it repeats only as long as the user doesn't exit the program with the "E" key.

Now, if you play with this program, you will see that it is a pretty basic calculator. It can't solve fancy algebra problem, but it can solve the basic mathematical question a child may need an answer for. In addition, this basic calculator can actually do a bit more than just solving simple multiplication and division. It can also perform what is called true division. Remember, that we discussed earlier about this topic which simply translates to whole number division. But, to refresh your memory, you know that normal division looks something like this: 9 / 2 = 4.5. This 4.5 result is obviously not a whole number, but is something that we can use in various programs or to solve other problems. But what if you are trying to figure out how many chocolates you can share equally with your friends, without giving more to someone? After all, nobody likes to feel left out because someone gets more chocolate that him. This means that we can't give someone extra chocolate.

If you have 2 friends and 9 pieces of chocolate to give them, you would have to cut a chocolate in half, so that each one gets 4.5 chocolates. Let's pretend you can't just cut one chocolate in half, so you would have to return it or give it to someone else. This would basically translate to long form division because 9 divided by 2 is equal to 4, and 1 as a remainder ($9 \div 2 = 4$ R1). Now, to perform integer division and not worry about remainders, all we need to do is use two forward slashes instead of one. In other words, in Python normal division looks like this:

$9 / 2 = 4.5$

And integer division looks like this:

$9 // 2 = 4$

$5 // 4 = 1$

As you can see, we don't get the remainder because we aren't interested in it in this example. All we want to know is how many chocolates we can share equally with our friends. However, if we do want the remainder, we can still calculate it separately. This is done by using what is called the modulo operator, symbolized in Python by the "%" symbol. Keep in mind that in Python % doesn't mean percent. If you want to write a percentage in Python you need to write it as a decimal number. So 10% in the real world becomes 0.1 in Python because the % symbol is the modulo operator, which is used to calculate the remainder. Therefore, if you want to find out the remainder from 9 / 2, then you write the following problem:

$9 \% 2 = 1$

$7 \% 4 = 3$

Simple, isn't it? Play around with your new calculator and you will see that every time you will get the correct result. And all it took was writing a handful of lines of code.

Summary

In this chapter you learned about variables and their data types. You learned that information can be stored in variables, and the type of variable is determined by the type of information. This includes numbers, whether integers or floating point numbers (decimals), as well as strings and lists. Storing this kind of information inside a variable makes your code cleaner and easier to read. By declaring variables you will be able to use it wherever you want in your program, as often as you want, without typing all that information all over again. Repetition is bad and you should avoid typing the same code more than twice. So, it's best to practice working with variables as soon as you learn what Python is.

In addition, you also learned how variables should be named. Naming conventions are important in programming, which means you should respect them. Don't forget that names are case sensitive, and it matters whether you choose to use underscores or compound words like "myVariable". No matter how you decide to name your variables, make sure to use the same naming technique throughout your code so that you avoid any confusion later on. Your programming friends will also appreciate this because it will make it easier for them to read and understand your code.

You also learned about all the mathematical operators you can use on integers and floating point numbers, as well as strings. Remember that some of them are different from those you use at school in math class. You need to use the right symbols that are recognized in programming languages instead. Furthermore, you learned how to work with strings and characters, and how some of those mathematical operators work even on them. You used the eval function for instance, to get Python to evaluate strings and determine when to use a certain number to perform a mathematical operation.

Then you explored the possibilities opened by lists. You learned how to use list variables and how you can store any type of variable or value in them. You also created an application that relies on lists to function properly. This type of variable is versatile and can be used in many situations, especially because they can contain any type of item or value.

Finally, you also learned about syntax errors, what they are, and why they occur. You will encounter them without a doubt, because no programmer is perfect no matter how many years of experience he or she has.

Ultimately, variables are essential to any program, and in time you will learn how to use each data type. You will practice working with them when you will create loops, or when you will learn how to write conditional statements. Variables are part of the computer's decision making process when it comes to applications, games, or more complex topics like designing artificial intelligence. Variables are the foundation of programming because they are used to simplify a complex problem by dividing it into a number of separate elements. You will see in time that the best approach to writing an application is by designing it in small parts that you work on one at a time.

With that being said, you now know how to work with the most fundamental programming tool, the variable. You are now prepared to learn about the next fundamental component that makes programming easier and more efficient, namely the function.

Chapter 3:

Functions

You have already worked with functions so far, but you probably don't fully understand what they are. You used various functions like print(), input(), and turtle.forward() to perform various actions, but you don't grasp the importance of functions and how they are used. The purpose of this chapter is to teach you what functions are all about and why you should always use this fundamental programming building block.

Functions are just that, building blocks. They are literally blocks of code that you define in the form of a function. That function is then activated only when we specifically call it inside our code. This already sounds pretty much like a variable, doesn't it? That's because functions follow the same structure, for the most part at least. You start by defining the function and declaring what information it will contain. Then you will use it throughout the code whenever you need it. The difference is that while a variable contains a value, a function contains a set of multiple values, variables, statements, loops and so on.

Until now, you have only used pre-defined functions. The functions mentioned earlier are already built into Python, or into Python modules like Turtle. This means that they already contain a set of commands and all you need to do is call for the function to do what it was designed to do. In this chapter, you will learn how to create your own function so that it can do whatever you want.

Functions are essential because they drastically reduce the amount of code we have to write. Instead of writing certain statements or loops multiple times throughout the program, we can define a function by storing those statements inside it. Then we can simply call the function whenever we need it. This means we will eliminate copy pasted code by reusing code we already have in the form of functions. It is much easier to write a set of statements once and then store them inside a function, because calling a function means writing a single word. Look at the pre-defined input() function for instance. All it does is print a prompt to the user to ask for an input. The user's input is then registered and processed by the application in the form of a string that is then stored inside a variable. This function can be used multiple times whenever we need to learn something from the user. Without it, we would have to perform each step that is part of the function, not once, but every single time we want information from the user. This would result in many unnecessary lines of code that would clutter and slow down our program.

Take another example, this time from the Turtle package, turtle.forward. This function allows us to draw our geometric shapes one pixel at a time in a specific direction, and by specifying the length of each line. Without having this function, we would need to be a bit creative and write a set of instructions that would color the pixels, calculate each location and angle, and perform some complex math in order to determine the distance on every update. This process alone would take a beginner a lot of time to design and then write in many lines of code.

Without having all of these functions, we would write dozens or even hundreds of additional lines of code. We would spend many hours figuring out small problems and writing code. Imagine writing such a program, and then returning to it a month later. You would probably need a few hours, or even days, to figure out what's going on. Functions remove all of this confusion. Plus, by having fewer lines of code, we will have fewer chances to mess things up and cause syntax errors to appear.

With that being said, let's learn how to define functions and make our code cleaner and easier to understand.

Defining Functions

The syntax of a function is simple. All we need to do is use the "def" keyword to define it and then insert any statements and instructions we want. Once the function is defined, we use its name to call it whenever we need it. Here's how a function definition looks in code:

Create a new Python file, save it and type:

def myFunction ():

print ("This functions says hello!")

That's it! Now we can call the function using its name like this in the IDLE shell window, then type enter :

myFunction()

Now imagine you have a block of code that you want to reuse. Let's say you want to draw a bunch of random shapes in random colors. You already have some of that code, but you probably already forgot some of it and you will need a bit of time to go back a few pages and remember how it all works. Take notice how easy it is to forget some code you wrote a while back, especially if it's been weeks. This is why you should use functions and make code reusable and easy to read. Functions can come in handy in not just one program, but multiple programs. So why write the same function several times when you can just extract it from one application and use it in another and save time?

We are going to declare a function that will generate a random spiral. Whenever we need to generate a spiral, like for a screen saver program, we can simply call this function. Don't forget that a function starts with the "def" keyword, which translates to "definition", followed by the function's name (something appropriate and easy to remember), parentheses and a colon. The function itself is going to be a collection of statements that will perform a number of actions. We will need to define the random color, size, as well as the screen location. Then we need to instruct the pen to move to that location and start drawing the spiral. All of these commands are inserted into one function definition and later when we want the spiral, we just use the function without having to write all of this information. With that being said, here's the code we need for the function:

Create a new Python file, save it and type:

```
import turtle

import random

p=turtle.Pen()

colors=["green", "blue", "yellow", "purple", "pink", "orange", "red", "violet"]

        def  randomSpiral():

                p.pencolor(random.choice(colors))

                size =  random.randint(10,40)

                x=random.randrange(-turtle.window_width()//2,
                turtle.window_width()//2)

                y=random.randrange(-turtle.window_height()//2,
                turtle.window_height()//2)

                p.penup()

                p.setpos(x,y)

                p.pendown()

                for m in range(size):

                        p.forward(m*2)

                        p.left(91)
```

(Source: **https://docs.python.org/3/library/turtle.html** retrieved in March 2021)

This is the time to Run the program via the menu Run>Run Module

Don't forget that after writing the function definition, the program will not run the function. This is just the definition. In order to execute all of this code, we need to call the function. By initiating the call, we command the computer to run all of these statements that the function contains. All we need to type is the following line:

randomSpiral()

Now we have a clean block of code that we can use whenever we want. We can even reuse this function in other applications, not just other parts of our code. This way the program will be easier to read and understand.

Another major benefit of using functions is the ability to share them online. Remember that teamwork is very important in programming and you will have to do a lot of research and talk to other programmers about your ideas, your programs and your code. By writing functions, you can immediately share them with others and they can use them in their own programs. You can also go online and find a function written by someone else to suit your own application. This will speed up your programming even more, because there's no need to reinvent the wheel. If it's out there on the Internet, you can find it and use it. But, before you start asking Google to find a solution to all of your programming problems, you should still learn how to solve them yourself.

Parameters

So far we have worked with simple pre-defined functions, and we created some of our own. However, when we define a function, we can also set a number of parameters for it. Parameters are there to add more information to the function, with the introduction of a series of arguments. This is what those empty parentheses are for in the function definition. So far we left them empty because we didn't have any arguments to add. However, if you remember your very first program, you will realize that you already used function parameters. In the first chapter you created your first "Hello, world!" program and in that code you used the print function. If you look at it again, you will see that you wrote the string "Hello, world!" inside the parentheses of the print function. That is a function argument, or parameter. In this case, the parameter represents a simple string.

Another example of a parameter can be found in our last application where we used the Turtle function p.left (90). In this case, the value of 90 represents how many degrees we want to move left. The randomSpiral function itself didn't hold any parameters however, because we wrote a collection of statements inside its definition, so there was no need for arguments.

To see functions in action, we are going to create a program that will draw a face somewhere on the computer screen. We will have a drawFace function that will draw the face at a random set of coordinates. This program will essentially do what the drawn shapes program did, however, it will be quite different because drawing a face requires more details. It won't be as simple as selecting a random color and size.

The best way to get started in this case is to grab a piece of paper and start using your creativity. Actually, you should do this no matter what program you are designing. Writing your ideas on paper and breaking down your large problems into smaller problems allows you to think more clearly and get better ideas. So let's start drawing this face one element at a time. Afterwards, we need to consider that the face will be generated anywhere on the screen, therefore we will be using coordinates. This means that the drawFace function will have two parameters, x and y, which will represent the coordinates where the face will appear. Now let's start from the very beginning by drawing the head first.

The generated faces will be created from a simple circle to represent the head, two smaller circles to represent the eyes, and some lines that will be the mouth. In order to do all of this we are going to have a reference point on the screen, and the drawFace function will generate all the shapes based on that point. But how do we start? This is the most complex program you have worked on so far and it is not enough to just think about it. It might sound overwhelming because you need to do a lot of things when writing the code. This is why you should grab a pen and a piece of paper and plan everything out. First you should plan how you will create the head, then the eyes and the mouth separately from each other.

To generate a face, we are going to start with the head first because it will serve as the canvas for the other shapes. But how big are we going to make the head? This is where drawing the head by hand on a piece of graph paper can come in handy. You can look at the paper and see how many lines the head covers. Then you can simply say that each line should translate to ten pixels in the program. Let's say that the head covers ten lines on paper, so that will mean 100 pixels on our screens. Keep in mind that because the head is a circle, the height and width will both be 100 pixels. This also means that the radius will be equal to 50 pixels. For this project we are going to use the Turtle module again, and we will need the radius value in order to use the circle function to draw the circle. This command takes the radius as its parameter, or argument and it will look something like this: p.circle (50). The function will draw the circle at the current coordinates, which will be 0 and 0. By equaling the x and y coordinates to zero, we will later be able to easily determine where to draw the eyes and the mouth.

Now we can decide which color to draw the head in. Let's pick red. You can make it any color you want, you simply need to specify it when declaring the pen. All you need to do is specify you want the fill color to be red by also specifying the paint fill option, not just the color of the pen. With all that being said, we are going to have a pen called "p" just like in earlier examples. Here's how the code for it and the face will look like:

Créer un nouveau fichier Python et sauvegardez-le, tapez le code et exécuter le module :

import turtle

p=turtle.Pen()

x=0

y=0

```
p.setpos(x,y)

p.pencolor ("red")

p.fillcolor ("red")

p.begin_fill()

p.circle (50)

p.end_fill()
```

(Source: **https://docs.python.org/3/library/turtle.html** retrieved in March 2021)

In this example you can again see why Python is so easy to work with. These lines of code are perfectly understandable because it's almost as if they are written in plain English. First we declare the color of the pen to be equal to red, then we also declare the fill color to be equal to red as well. Next, we use the circle keyword to create the face with a radius equal to 50 pixels. Once the circle is created, it will be filled with color. The fill function is used for this process.

Now that we have the face, we can start working on the details. What we need first is the eyes, but we need to think where to place them so that they don't look awkward. We are going to generate the left eye first, and then fill it with color. Since the face is 100 pixels in size, we are going to make the eye smaller, let's say twenty pixels. Again, we are going to create circles for the eyes, so we need to use the circle function again and declare the radius parameter, which in this case will be a value of ten (half of twenty). The only problem here is figuring out the location for the eyes. The coordinates we determined so far are the reference point for the face. Again, our hand drawing on graph paper can come in handy here as well. If we look at our drawing we can see how many lines we have above the original coordinates. Let's say that we are placing the left eye six lines above the original point that determined the location of the face. Six lines are equal to sixty pixels, therefore we are going to move sixty pixels upwards. This is the positive y-direction. If you haven't studied much math or geometry yet, don't worry too much about this. Just remember that the positive y direction, or axis, means going up. The left eye will also be 15 pixels to the left, which is the negative x axis.

To write all of this in code is actually easier than it seems. The brainstorming phase and the hand drawing might seem like it takes some time, but getting prepared will make our jobs easier. What we determined is that we need to draw the left eye starting from the original reference point of the face, and move 15 pixels to the left and another 60 pixels upwards. This means we will move 15 pixels on the x coordinate, and 60 pixels on the y coordinate. To do this we need to use the "setpos" command that takes the two coordinates as parameters. Here's how the code for the left eye of the face will look:

In the same Python file, type the following code, run the module and save:

p.setpos (x − 15, y + 60)

p.fillcolor ("yellow")

p.begin_fill()

p.circle (10)

p.end_fill ()

(Source: **https://docs.python.org/3/library/turtle.html** retrieved in March 2021)

As you can see the code is identical to what we wrote for the face drawing. The only exception is the setpos function. Pay attention to it in particular and see how we wrote this command. We didn't just write the coordinates like we did when generating the face. If we would type -15 and 60 as values, instead of x − 15 and y +60 we wouldn't be able to generate other faces properly at the same time because the eyes would always have the same coordinates. Therefore, we would end up with faces without eyes. Only our initial face drawing has x and y equal to 0. Other faces will use different coordinates. By declaring x -15 and y + 60 we tell the program to subtract 15 pixels and add 60 pixels to the two coordinates no matter what they are. This way new faces will always have their own eyes.

Now that we have the left eye, we need to draw the right eye as well. You can do this on your own as a small challenge. The code will be the same, with a small difference regarding the position of the eye. It will still be 60 pixels up from the base coordinates, but instead of being 15 pixels to the left of the original point, it will be 15 pixels to the right. So, all you need to do is write the same code as for the left eye, but change the setpos function like this:

p.setpos (x + 15, y + 60)

Now that our face has eyes, let's create the mouth. We are going to make the face smile, because nobody likes a grumpy face. To do this, we will use lines instead of circles, namely three lines. Let's turn to our hand drawing and draw a mouth to see how it will look approximately and determine the coordinates. Let's say that the side of the mouth will be 20 pixels to the left and 35 pixels above the reference point of the face. This means we need to set the position to be equal to x -20 and y + 35. Next, we need to decide the color of the mouth and how thick the lines should be. Let's make the lines 8 pixels in width and color them blue. What's important, however, is to properly manage the position of the mouth, since we are drawing a smile. We need to start generating the mouth from the left side, so we will start with x – 10, y +20, go to x + 10, y + 20 and then x +20, y +35. You can play with these values until you have the smile you want. It can be more symmetric, or less, depending on what you find more hilarious or interesting. Now let's see the actual code for the mouth:

p.setpos (x -20, y + 35)

p.pencolor ("blue")

p.width (8)

p.goto (x – 10, y + 20)

p.goto (x + 10, y + 20)

p.goto (x + 20, y + 35)

p.width(1)

(Source: **https://docs.python.org/3/library/turtle.html** retrieved in March 2021)

As you can see, we placed the starting point in the upper left corner of the smile, declared the color of the pen to be blue, and the width of its line to be 8 pixels. Then we used the goto() function to tell the pen where to move in order to draw the mouth. This function works exactly the same as setpos() in principle. It simply moves the pen to the coordinates we declare as the parameters. The last line of the code will thin the line back to one pixel so that the mouth isn't too thick when we create all the other faces.

Now that we have all the components to generate the face, we can create the drawFace function so that we can implement a loop inside it that will create fifty random coordinates where a face will be generated. We will need the x and y coordinates for the function as the arguments so that we can establish where to create each face. There is one other problem we need to keep in mind here. Between each face, we need to tell the program to lift the pen. When you draw something on a piece of paper, you don't just go with a continuous line, do you? You lift your hand to remove the pen from the paper, and then place it somewhere else on the paper where you draw some more. Python doesn't do this automatically. As the programmer, you need to tell your program every single step it needs to take. Therefore, you need to write code that will tell the application to lift the pen once a face is drawn, in order to move the pen to another location and draw a new face. With that in mind, let's take a look at the code:

```
def drawFace (x,y):

p.penup()

p.setpos(x,y)

p.pendown()
```

(Source: **https://docs.python.org/3/library/turtle.html** retrieved in March 2021)

Now we can place all of the code for the face drawing here in the drawFace function. All the blocks of code we wrote for the face, eyes, and mouth needs to be placed here in our new function. And, we can add a loop so that we create fifty new locations for more faces to be generated. This is what the code will look like with the loop:

```
import turtle
import random
p=turtle.Pen()
def drawFace():
    for n in range(50):
            x=random.randrange(-turtle.window_width()//2,turtle.window_width()//2)
            y=random.randrange(-turtle.window_height()//2,turtle.window_height()//2)
            p.pencolor("")
            p.setpos(x,y)
            p.pencolor("red")
            p.fillcolor("red")
            p.begin_fill()
            p.circle(50)
            p.end_fill()
            p.setpos(x-15,y+60)
            p.fillcolor("yellow")
            p.begin_fill()
            p.circle(10)
            p.end_fill()
            p.setpos(x+15,y+60)
            p.fillcolor("yellow")
            p.begin_fill()
            p.circle(10)
            p.end_fill()
            p.setpos(x-20,y+35)
            p.pencolor("blue")
            p.width(8)
            p.goto(x-10,y+20)
            p.goto(x+10,y+20)
            p.goto(x+20,y+35)
            p.width(1)
```

(Source: **https://docs.python.org/3/library/turtle.html** retrieved in March 2021)

We can now call the function using its name, like this in the IDLE shell window and type enter:

drawFace ()

Here you go!

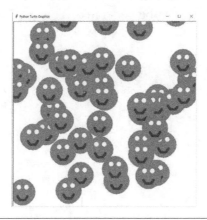

All we're doing here is generating random x and y coordinates to create locations from the left side of the program window to the right, and from downwards to upwards. These random locations are then introduced as parameters to the drawFace function so that a face can be drawn at each set of coordinates.

That's it! But wait, there's more! Before you continue reading this book to learn cool new things, you should take a break and play around with this program. You can modify in many ways without learning anything new and draw whatever shape you want. You can change the coordinates, the lines, the colors, and any other feature of the shape we have drawn in this example. You can even use this program as inspiration and write a new one from scratch. Design a new shape using your imagination. Just remember to start with a pen and paper, and preferably graph paper, so you can easily break your idea into small parts that you write individually in code. The graph paper will also help you come up with good dimensions for each shape and with proportions. After all, you don't want to make the mouth larger than half of the face. Or maybe you do? Unleash your creative side and see how Python can make a designer and an artist out of you, not just a programmer who writes plain code.

Returning Values

Now that you have a basic understanding of functions and parameters, you need to know that you can also obtain data from a function, not just send it and store it. For instance, let's say we want to create a program that can convert kilograms to pounds and we want to save that converted value so that we can work with it in other operations. Until now, we only printed such values directly, but in the real world we will need to use those values in other parts of the program. This is where the return statement comes in. It allows us to send data from a function to any other section of our application.

There are many situations where we will need to gain data from functions. As mentioned just now, any program that converts values will require the use of return statements. Let's create such a program and give it the ability to transform inches to centimeters. The inch value will become the parameter of a function in this case, because functions can send data back to the program. This data will be the value in centimeters instead of inches. In order to perform this conversion process, all we need to do is multiply the inches we have by the value of 2.54. One inch is equal to approximately 2.54 centimeters. Now to return this centimeter value, we will use a return statement. This works by using the return keyword and a value which will be sent back to the program as a result to be used in other situations. Let's start by defining the function, and then returning the value:

```
def conversionToCentimeters (numberOfInches):

return numberOfInches * 2.54
```

You can try this out in a *shell*, without creating a program. Using these lines of code, type conversionToCentimeters (10) and then hit the "enter" button on your keyboard. Python will automatically perform the conversion of 10 inches into a value in centimeters. All you need to do is replace the "numberOfInches" with an actual value to perform the calculation. The value is then returned by the function, and we can see it printed in the *shell*. You can create other small conversion programs like this. For instance, you can convert feet to meters, or pounds to kilograms. All you need to do is look up the base value of 1 pound or 1 foot, and then replace the values in the program we just wrote with the appropriate values for those measurements. As a small exercise, you should create another little program that converts pounds to kilograms. We will use that code snipped later on to create a real application. Just follow the same structure of the little program we already created.

You will notice that the return statement is like using function arguments, but backwards. The only difference is that we only have one value instead of multiple parameters.

Let's use all of this information to create another fun program using conversions and return statements. We are going to create an application that will calculate our weight and height in coconuts. Yes, we can measure anything we want in coconuts because… why not? With a bit of imagination and Python knowledge we can pretty much do anything we want. So, let's start by doing a little bit of research and find out what is the average weight of a coconut and its average diameter. With a bit of help from Google, we will learn that the average weight of a coconut is roughly 680 grams, or 24 ounces, and the average diameter is 7 inches, or roughly 18cm. In order to determine how many coconuts will be equal to our weight and height, we have to divide our height measured in centimeters by 18, and then divide our weight in grams by 680. But now we arrive at another problem. Not everyone measures their weight in grams and their height in inches. Luckily, the two small conversion programs we discussed earlier will come in handy. We can convert all of that data to any system we need. Then we can take those values and perform another conversion, but this time in units measured in coconuts.

The coconut conversion program will require the definition for the two functions, namely conversionToCentimeters, and conversionToKilograms. The next step will be asking the user to input his or her height and weight in coconuts and then print the calculations. Here's how the code would look:

Create a new Python file, save it, type the code below and run the module:

```
def conversionToCentimeters (numberOfInches):

        return numberOfInches * 2.54

def conversionToKilograms (numberOfPounds):

        return numberOfPounds / 2.2

heightInches = int (input ("How tall are you in inches: "))

weightPounds = int (input ("How much do you weight in pounds: "))

heightCentimeters = conversionToCentimeters (heightInches)

weightKilograms = conversionToKilograms (weightPounds)

coconutsTall = round (heightCentimeters / 18)

coconutsHeavy = round (weightKilograms * 1000 / 680)

feet = heightInches // 12

inch = heightInches % 12

print ("At", feet, "feet", inch, "inches tall, and ", weightPounds, "pounds")

print ("you measure", coconutsTall, "Coconuts tall, and ")

print (" you weight ", coconutsHeavy, "Coconuts!")
```

```
def conversionToCentimeters (numberOfInches):
    return numberOfInches * 2.54
def conversionToKilograms (numberOfPounds):
    return numberOfPounds / 2.2

heightInches = int (input("How tall are you in inches: "))
weightPounds = int (input("How much do you weight in pounds: "))
heightCentimeters = conversionToCentimeters (heightInches)
weightKilograms = conversionToKilograms (weightPounds)
coconutsTall = round (heightCentimeters / 18)
coconutsHeavy = round (weightKilograms * 1000 / 680)
feet = heightInches // 12
inch = heightInches % 12
print ("At", feet, "feet", inch, "inches tall, and ", weightPounds, "pounds")
print ("you measure", coconutsTall, "Coconuts tall, and ")
print ("you weight ", coconutsHeavy, "Coconuts!")
```

The first step is to insert the two conversion code snippets we discussed earlier. These functions rely on input parameters and they each return a value. In the next stage, the program will ask the user to type in his or her weight and height. These values are then stored inside the heightInches and weightPounds variables. Next, the first conversion function is called in order to pass the heightInches variable as the value that needs to be converted. Then the value is stored in a new variable called heightCentimeters. The next step is about yet another conversion which relies on the convertToKilograms function in order to convert a user's weight from pounds to kilograms.

The next part of the program involves an equation. The height of the user will be divided by 18 in order to determine the height in coconuts. Keep in mind that the result will be rounded to the nearest whole number in order to keep things simple. This process is done with the help of the round() function. This result is then stored in a new variable called coconutsTall. The next step is similar because it involves the same type of equation in order to convert the user's weight into grams from kilograms, and then divide that result by 680, which represents the average weight of a coconut. Again, we round the result in order to keep things simple and easy to read and then we store it a new variable called coconutHeavy.

We are almost done, but we still need to do a bit of math. After all the above, we need to determine the user's height in both feet and inches because that's how many people measure themselves. Therefore, let's give those users that option in case they don't like the metric system. In order to achieve that we use the // operator we discussed earlier in order to perform integer division. Then we store the result in a new variable called "feet". Then we use the modulo operator in order to find out the remainder, which will be measured in inches. As you can see, this is a perfect real world example where the modulo operator and integer division can come in handy.

Finally, we have a series of print statements that will print the user's height and weight in normal measurement units, as well as in coconuts. That's it! Now you can tell your friends how many coconuts you weight. With a bit of research you can write other conversion programs in which you use any outlandish unit of measurement you want. You can learn how many tennis balls or chocolate chip cookies you weight. Let your imagination go wild, take notes, plan your application and then practice practice practice!

Quiz ? ☺

It's quiz time! Let's test what you have learned so far. Once you have answered all the questions, go to the final chapter to see the results and compare!

1. Which function will print an output to the screen?

echo

print

eval

2. What is the output of this code:

```
def x():
        pass
print (type (f()))
```

3. What is the purpose of the following code:

```
def a (b, c, d):
        pass
```

4. What's the output of the following block of code:

```
a = [1,2,3,None,(),[],]
print (len(a))
```

4

5

6

5. State the value of the item with index 1 from the following list:

colors = ['red', 'orange', 'yellow', 'green', 'blue', 'indigo', 'violet']

red

orange

violet

6. Is the statement "There are only two value types in Python, strings and numbers" correct?

True

False

7. What is the result of this code: num = '5'*'5'

333

5

Type Error

8. What is the result of this code: print (abc)

"abc"

abc

Error

9. Is the statement "There are only two types of numbers in Python, assigned values and integers" correct?

True

False

10. What is the result of this code: print (3 //5)

0.6

0

None

Summary

In this chapter you learned about the importance of functions and how useful they can be. They are one of the fundamental building blocks of all applications and no programmer can survive for long without them. They are used to make your code reusable within the same program, or even other programs. With the help of functions you can call a set of statements anywhere in your program. You can even share your functions with other programmers, and you can use those that are written by others in online Python programming communities.

In this chapter you have also learned about parameters and their purpose inside functions. This allows you to create more complex programs. As you progress you will see that functions will become truly mandatory and you will often use parameters. This is especially the case when you start working on creating games. In addition, return statements will also become the norm because you will often use them to gain information from the functions in the form of return values.

With everything you learned in this chapter, you are now ready to learn more advanced topics. You know enough about Python programming to create a variety of simple and useful apps, but in order to create truly powerful programs, you need to learn more. In the meantime, you should keep practicing the concepts you've learned so far. Get used to turning your code into reusable functions so that you can work faster, more efficiently, and be able to share ideas with your friends.

There's still a lot of material to study but so far you have accomplished quite a lot. Here's what you know how to do so far:

1. Define functions so that you avoid copy pasting code throughout your programs.

2. Call your custom functions from any other applications.

3. Pass parameters to your functions and return values that you can use for various operations.

4. Write programs that can convert any values into other values.

5. Work with mathematical coordinates and functions in order to navigate through space and draw various pictures.

As you can see, you learned quite a lot. So take a break, go back to the beginning of the chapter, read once again through the material and create some programs of your own. Functions will be used throughout this book and in real world game and application development. So take your time and study well, but don't forget to also be creative and have fun!

Chapter 4:

Loops

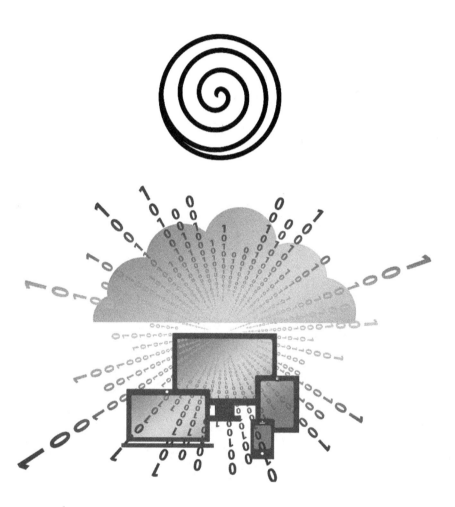

You are already somewhat familiar with loops because we had to use them a couple of times to make our programs work the way we wanted them to. We used them to repeatedly draw shapes or generate new coordinates for our face drawing program. However, you haven't truly learned yet how they work. In this chapter we are going to focus on learning how to create loops and which types of loops to use.

The basic idea behind loops is fairly simple. When we need to repeat something inside an application, we can use a loop. By doing so we will no longer need to write a certain code block multiple times. The loop will keep repeating any set of commands.

Imagine having a program that draws certain shapes that overlap each other. Let's take a circle for instance because you are already familiar with the circle() function from the Turtle package. This function draws a circle based on the radius parameter we declare in the parentheses. Let's say we create four overlapping circles, placed in each of the four directions on our screen. They are 90 degrees apart and we can make them turn. To do all of this we could write four separate blocks of code in order to draw each circle, then turn it and then create another circle. Here's how this simple code looks:

```
import turtle

p = turtle.Pen()

# this will make the circle point upwards

p.circle (100)

# now the circle will be turned by 90 degrees to the left

p.left (90)

# now let's create the second circle

p.circle (100)

# and also turn it by 90 degrees to the left and make it point to the left side of the screen

p.left (90)

# next we create the third circle and make it point downwards

p.circle (100)
```

p.left (90)

and finally we create the fourth circle that will point to the right

p.circle (100)

p.left (90)

(Source: https://docs.python.org/3/library/turtle.html retrieved in March 2021)

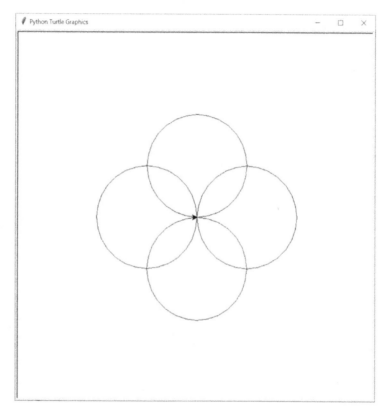

Looks extremely boring doesn't it? The code does indeed work just fine, but it is incredibly repetitive and inefficient. We have too many lines of code that simply do the same thing four times. We already discussed earlier that we shouldn't repeat the same code more than twice. Instead, we can make the block of code reusable by introducing a for loop. Let's talk more about for loops and why they're so great.

For Loops

Simply put, a "for" loop iterates over any type of sequence, whether it's a string or a list. This means that we can execute any number of statements for each item in the list or character in a string. Here's a very basic example of how a for loop works:

shoppingList = ["potatoes", "flour", "butter"]

for x in shoppingList:

print (x)

You will notice that each item in this list will be printed in a new line. We don't have to write three different print statements, instead, we can just use the loop to run through the entire list and print each item individually.

In order to create our loops, we need to first think about which steps need to be repeated multiple times. Returning to the example at the beginning of this chapter, the repeating instructions are essentially the p.circle (100) declaration used to generate a circle, and the p.left (90) function that turns the circle before a new one is generated. The next step is to decide how many times we need to repeat this set of instructions. In this example, we're interested in four circles, therefore we need a loop that repeats itself four times.

Once we've answered both of these questions we can start writing the for loop. As mentioned earlier, this type of loop will iterate over any list of objects, and repeat a set of instructions for each one. In our example, we want to repeat the loop four times, therefore we need a list with four items. This list will actually contain numbers in this case, so we are going to use the "range" function in order to generate the number list. Here's how this function is used:

range (10)

We need to declare a parameter for this function that will establish how many numbers it will generate. In this case it will create a sequence of numbers from 0 to 9. Why not to 10 you ask? In programming, numbering starts from 0, not from

1. Zero doesn't mean nothing in programming languages. It actually means the first element, or one. Therefore, 0 1 2 3 4 5 6 7 8 9 is a collection of 10 numbers. Now, in order to test this function and list these numbers, you can launch the command prompt window and type the following line of code:

list (range (5))

This will print an output containing a list of 5 numbers going from 0 to 4. Change the number inside the parentheses in order to make the list shorter or longer.

Since for our little program we need to draw four shapes, we will use a range of four elements in order to do so. The loop itself will start like this:

for x in range(4)

The "for" keyword determine the type of the loop. Then we have "x" which is a variable that acts as the counter. Next, we have the "in" keyword which instructs the variable to count through a given range list. Finally, we have the range function that establishes a list of numbers for the loop to iterate through, in this case a list equal to [0, 1, 2, 3]. Now let's recreate the program we wrote at the beginning of the chapter by using a for loop instead of repeating so many lines of code:

```
import turtle

p = turtle.Pen ()

for x in range(4):

        p.circle (100)

        p.left (90)
```

(Source: https://docs.python.org/3/library/turtle.html retrieved in March 2021)

That's it! See how much shorter the program is? It's still not a very exciting program because it doesn't do much, but at least it wasn't that tedious to write it. Thanks to the for loop we have obtained the same results, but now we have a cleaner code and we didn't waste any time typing it out.

Now that you understand how the for loop works, start thinking about how to modify your program to fit 8 circles instead of four. Give it some thought and think what needs to change in order to accommodate twice the circles.

Hopefully you came up with some ideas of your own and you tried to rework the program. You already know everything you need to work it out. However, if you didn't manage, you probably missed something in your logic. Not to worry, it happens to the best of us. Let's figure this out together.

First, we know that the new program requires eight circles. This means that the first change we have to make is to the range function. We need a range of 8 items to create our new for loop. But that is not enough. If that is the only change we're making, then we will see no difference when the shapes are printed to our screen. Why is that? Remember that 90 degree rotation? Having four times 90 degree rotations we end up with a total of 360 degrees. Therefore, when we have eight 90 degree rotations, we just end up with another set of 4 circles that overlap the previous four, so we won't see any difference. To fix this we need to change the rotation value. To do so, we just need to divide 360, because that is the total we can have around the center, by 8 because we will have eight circles. 360 / 8 = 45 degrees. This means that each turn will be made at 45 degrees in order to fit 8 circles. Therefore, the p.left() function will have a parameter with the value of 45 instead of 90. Here's how the code will look now:

```
import turtle

p = turtle.Pen()

for x in range (8):

        p.circle (100)

        p.left (45)
```

(Source: https://docs.python.org/3/library/turtle.html retrieved in March 2021)

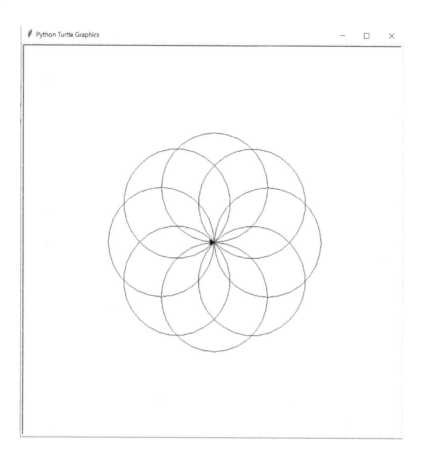

In this version of the program, the loop statement will iterate through a list of 8 numbers going from 0 to 7. This means that the two statements will be executed 8 times. The main difference between this program and the previous one is the fact that the circles turn 45 degrees at a time instead of 90. This way we end up seeing 8 circles generated around a central point. This makes quite a pretty illustration, and fortunately we didn't have to write all of the commands 8 times for each circle individually. That would be very time consuming, not to mention boring and tedious. But we can improve this program even further and make it more interesting and fun!

Fun with For Loops

Let's make our circle generating program a bit more interesting by giving the user the ability to type any number and based on that number, a collection of circles will be drawn automatically. We can make this application more interactive by calculating how any number of circles needs to be arranged so that all of them are neatly stacked around the central point on your screen. The first thing we need to do is determine that the range of numbers is equal to the number which the user types. Once the program has the input, it needs to simply divide the 360 degrees by that value in order to obtain the number of degrees each circle needs to turn when iterating through the loop. Let's take a look at the code and see what happens:

```
import turtle

p = turtle.Pen()
```

We are going to ask the user to type how many circle he or she wants the program to generate. We will also leave a default value of 8, just in case the user doesn't want to input any number.

```
totalShapes = int (turtle.numinput ("Total number of shapes", "How many shapes do you want?", 8))

for x in range (totalShapes):

        p.circle (100)

        p.left (360 / totalShapes)
```

(Source: https://docs.python.org/3/library/turtle.html retrieved in March 2021)

Let's break down what we have in this application. First, we create a new variable called "totalShapes" that will use some functions. As before, we are also using the Turtle package so that we have access to the numinput() function, which is used to allow the program to ask a user for a numeral input. Next, we have a couple of strings that are printed for the user, followed by the value of 8. This value is important because if the user doesn't specify how many circles he wants to generate, the program will create 8. The input from the user is then stored as an integer so that it can be used in the range function. Next, we have the for loop which relies on the totalShapes variable in order to iterate through a list of values equal to that variable's value. The instructions to draw the shape remain exactly the same as before. The major difference is the fact that we divide the total value of 360 degrees by the number which the user inputs. This way the program determines automatically how many circles it can display by adjusting the angle value. For instance, if you specify you want 20 circles, each circle will turn by 18 degrees, because 360 / 20 = 18.

Have fun with this program by inputting any number to see what happens. You can generate hundreds of circles. Just keep in mind that if you go with a large number, you will have to wait for Python to process each iteration of the loop and draw all those circles. You can also use everything else you learned so far to make other changes to the program. For example, you can change the color of the background. You can also change the color of the circle's line. You can choose to draw squares instead of circles. You can make the circles grow in size gradually. There's no limit to what you can do with a bit of imagination and a bit of Python.

While Loops

The for loop is versatile and useful in any kind of program, however, it's not an almighty solution that can be used to solve any problem. It has limits. For example, let's say we need to stop the loop from running when something happens in the program. We don't always want to go through the entire loop. Or let's say we can't figure out how many times we should execute a certain loop. This is especially the case when designing games because it's impossible for us to know how many times a certain player will want to perform an action. So we need to allow them to always choose whenever they want, without any limits that will require them to restart the game. Just imagine forcing your friends to quit their game or shut down their console and restart it before being able to play another round. Nobody would like to go through that.

In order to solve all the problems mentioned above, we need to introduce a different type of loop into our programs. The solution to many of these issues is the "while" loop. While this also falls in the category of loops, it functions completely differently from the for loop. Instead of running through a list of items or numbers, the while loop simply looks whether a condition is met, and based on that condition it decides whether it repeats itself or quits running. In other words, while something is true, something will happen. When it's no longer true, that action will end and the program will continue with the next commands. With that being said, here's how the syntax looks:

while condition:

    type statements here

The while condition is simply a true or false test. This is also known as a Boolean expression because we can only have two values here. Either something is true or it's false. There are no other options. Here's the while statement in a more easy to understand example: while hungry, eat. While you are hungry, you will continue eating, therefore going through a loop of putting food in your mouth, chewing it, and swallowing it. When you are no longer hungry, you will stop eating, therefore exit the loop, and continue with your day.

Another important aspect of while loops are the comparison operators. When we write a while loop, we will sometimes have to compare values in order to execute a certain block of code. This is especially true when working with numbers. For instance, we might have something like the following logic: If x is smaller than 10, execute this line of code. When x is no longer smaller than 10, the code will stop executing. This translates to the following: while x < 10 is true, do something. The "<" symbol means lesser than and is known as a comparison operator because it compares at least 2 values. Other such comparison operators are ">" (greater than), "==" (equal to), "<=" (lesser or equal to), ">=" (greater or equal to) and "!=" (not equal to). Pay special attention to the equal to comparison operator because it is written with double equal signs. This is important, because typing one equal means that we are declaring a certain value to a variable, instead of comparing two values.

There are, however, some similar characteristics that the while loop shares with the for loop. For instance, both loops will repeat a collection of instructions as many times as required. Both loops will also tell Python to execute only the statements that belong to them. With that being said, let's take a look at a simple program to see how while loops work in practice:

tell the user to input his or her name

name = input ("what's your name?")

---

the name will be displayed until we exit the program

while name != "":

#print the name 50 times

    for x in range (50):

        print (name, end = " ")

    print ()

ask the user to type a new name

or quit the program

    name = input ("type a new name, or hit the [ENTER] key to quit the program")

    print ("see you later!")

File Edit Format Run Options Window Help

```
name = input ("what's your name?")
while name!=" ":
    for x in range(50):
        print(name,end=" ")
    print (" ")
    name = input ("type a new name, or hit the [ENTER] key to quit the program ")
    print ("see you later!")
```

Let's discuss what we did in more detail. First, just like in one of our first programs, we ask the user to type his or her name. This name will then be stored inside a variable, which will be used in a test where we will check for it as a condition in a while loop. When we enter the loop, it will start executing for as long as the user's name input is different from an empty string with no names. This empty string is written as two quotation marks with no character inside them. Next, we have a for loop in our application as well. Its purpose is to print the user's name 50 times, each time with a space to separate them. As usual, the for loop will repeat itself whenever x is under the value of 50, which is the maximum of the range we declared. When we reach 50 prints, the program will print an empty line, and then ask the user to type a new name. If a new name is entered, the program starts running from the while loop all over again, performing each step like before. As long as we don't have an empty string as the input, the program will run the for loop to print the new name 50 times. When we eventually do have an empty string, the program will stop executing by ending the loop and saying goodbye to the user.

This simple program is a perfect example of how we can use the two different loops together to perform a different set of actions. Each one of them fulfills a different purpose.

Let's now use all the previous knowledge we gathered so far, together with the idea of printing a list of names to the screen, and create something more interesting. We are going to mix the name printing loop together with a shape generating program similar to what we've already created. We will build a spiral shape object that is made out of a list of names. One of the most important aspects we need to brainstorm in this case is how to repeat the names at the same time in order to draw the shape. We can't just print that one at a time because that wouldn't look interesting and would take some time to be processed. What we need to do is create a list and keep every name we're going to use for the shape in that list. This is similar to what we did in an earlier project by using a list of colors. Then, as the loop is being executed, the names will change. Our spiral will have several branches, so we are going to dedicate one name per branch, as well as one color. That way, all the corners of the shape will consist of a separate name and color.

Now, let's start by first declaring a list with no items in it:

myFriends = []

This list will hold names of your friends. Remember that when we used a list of colors in our previous examples we already knew the colors we wanted to use. In this case, however, we want the user to type in the names he or she wants instead of having pre-determined names. By having a blank list with nothing but a pair of brackets, we tell Python that we want a list called "myFriends", but the objects will only be known when the application is running.

Now that we have a blank list, we are going to use a while loop like we did earlier in order to ask for the user's chosen names. Those names will then be added to the empty list. The user will type a name, and it will become the first item of the list. When he types another name, it will become the second element, after the first name. The user can add as many names as he wants. When they are all added, the "enter" key will be pressed in order to let the application know that we are finished introducing list items. At this point, we are going to introduce a for loop to our program in order to take care of the artistic drawing. This is where the shapes will be created using the names from the list. Now, let's see how the code will look:

```
import turtle

p = turtle.Pen ()

turtle.bgcolor ("white")

myColors = ["purple", "green", "blue", "red", "yellow", "black", "pink", "brown", "orange", "teal"]

myFriends = []

typeName = turtle.textinput ("My friends", "Type the names of your friends and hit the [ENTER] key to continue")

while typeName != "":

myFriends.append (typeName)

typeName = turtle.textinput ("My friends", "Type the names of your friends and then press [ENTER] to continue")

for x in range (10):

        p.pencolor (myColors [x%len(myFriends)])

        p.penup ()

        p.forward (x * 4)

        t.pendown()

        p.write (myFriends [x%len(myFriends)])

        font = ("Arial", int((x+4)/4), "bold")

        p.left (360/len (myFriends) + 2)
```

```
import turtle
p=turtle.Pen()
turtle.bgcolor("white")
myColors =["purple", "green", "blue", "red", "yellow", "black", "pink", "brown", "orange", "teal"]
myFriends =[]
typeName = turtle.textinput ("My friends", "Type the names of your friends and hit the [ENTER] key to continue")
while typeName !="":
    myFriends.append(typeName)
    typeName = turtle.textinput ("My friends", "Type additional names of your friends and hit the [ENTER] key to continue")
    for x in range (10):
        p.pencolor (myColors [x%len(myFriends)])
        p.penup ()
        p.forward (x * 4)
        p.pendown()
        p.write(myFriends[x%len(myFriends)])
        font=("Arial",int((x+4)/4),"bold")
        p.left(360/len(myFriends)+2)
```

(Source: https://docs.python.org/3/library/turtle.html retrieved in March 2021)

Phew, this program is a bit more complicated than the others we worked on so far, but don't worry, we are going to break it down. On a side note, when you don't fully understand a program, you should start breaking in into small parts. Don't analyze it as an entire application because it's easy to get lost then. Read one line at a time and think about each one. Analyze them individually, and when you understand what's going on, move to the next line. When you can't understand a certain line of code, break that into smaller pieces as well and look at them one at a time. You will eventually realize that you simply don't know what one or two keywords mean. But once you know what you don't understand, you can research it quickly and find out. As mentioned earlier, working with code is no different from playing with Legos. All you do is use small bits to create blocks which you then use to create an entire object. With that being said, let's go back to our code and see what's going on.

First, we create the blank list as mentioned earlier. We called it "myFriends" and it will contain all the names of the user's friends once he enters them while the application is running. After the first name is registered, the while loop will keep running until all the names are gathered. At the end of this process, we have an "append" function, which takes each name that was typed by the user and adds it to the list in proper order. All names are added one after each other in the blank list, in the same order the user types them. Then when the user hits the "enter" key, the program will know that he is done typing names.

This is where the for loop comes in. Just like before, we declare the color of the pen first. You will also notice that we have a new keyword here called "len". This keyword stands for length and it determines how long the list of names is. For instance, if the user types five names, the "len" command will return five.

Next, the modulo operator is used so that we can cycle through five colors. Each color will match one of the names. The more names we have, the more color rotations we will have. However, this is limited to ten colors, because that's all we added to our list of colors. If you want more options, simply add more colors to the list. In this loop we also use the "penup" function in order to move the pen away from the screen so that it doesn't generate any drawings when we move it forward to the next shape. If we didn't use this, we would have lines connecting everything. Remember, in programming, you need to tell everything what you want the program to do because it won't decide for itself like you do. Next, the pen is placed down again in order to generate more names.

In the next phase, the pen will be told what to draw specifically. We have a sort of formula here that looks like this [x%len(myFriends)]. What this means is that we are using the modulo operator to cycle through the entire list of names and then process them in the order they were added. Then we specify the font we want the names to be written in. Here we used Arial, and then we made it bold, but you can use other fonts as well, like Times New Roman, or fancier ones like Gothic. You can also make the writing Italic instead of bold. Or why not both?

Another modification we made in order to make the drawings more interesting is the following declaration that makes the font size grow.

The (x + 4) /4 line means that when the loop reaches 10, or x = 10, the size of the font will be increased. You can play around with these values to see what happens. You can make the font go smaller in size, or even bigger. Lastly, we write another equation that tells the pen to go left by a "360 / len (myFriends)" amount of degrees plus another two. This means that if we have 4 friends in the list, they will rotate 90 degrees each, plus another two, so that the shapes form a neat spiral. Remember from the past example where we discussed degrees that the more items we have, the fewer degrees they will rotate. A list of 8 names will rotate 45 degrees + 2, instead of 90 + 2, and so on. The purpose of those 2 additional degrees is to make the shapes go to the left in order to create a cool whirlpool effect.

Nested Loops

So far we've seen how useful and necessary for and while loops are, but we've only used them briefly. They handled our repetitive code beautifully and spared us the boredom of writing dozens of nearly identical lines of code. However, they can do even more by forming nested loops.

Nested loops are simply loops inside other loops and we can repeat this as much as we want. We can create an entire chain of loops inside other loops that are inside other loops, and so on. In order to easily understand this concept, we are going to go back to drawing. Visual art is great at explaining boring theory, so we will stick to using the turtle package and drawing more spirals and other geometrical shapes. However, this time, we won't draw a series of names that will form a shape, we will draw a spiral built out of spirals.

To do this, we are going to have one loop that will draw the main spiral. Then we will write another loop inside the main loop. Its purpose will be drawing all the tiny spirals that will form the large one. But before we get to that, let's talk more about nested loops and how they look in code.

To write a nested loop, we need to start as usual, by writing a loop. Once we have the loop, we leave some empty space and type the next loop. Starting the line after the initial loop with some space tells Python that the next statement belongs to that loop. This works exactly like it did with all the other statements that we wrote inside other for and while loops. Nested loops are just statements that belong to other loops, even though they are loops themselves. Now let's look at some code because you are probably confused:

```
for x in range (100):

    for y in range (100):
```

The first loop wraps itself around the nested loop. Keep in mind that sometimes the main loop that holds everything is known as the outer loop, and the loops that are nested inside it are known as inner loops. With that being said, the inner loop will be executed 100 times, and the main loop will also be executed 100 times. This means a total of 100 * 100 executions.

Now, let's start writing our new program to fully understand how nested loops can be used in the real world. Since this application may sound a bit confusing due to all the loops inside other loops, we are going to discuss each step we take. Now, let's start as usual, by importing turtle and setting up the turtle pen:

```
import turtle

p = turtle.Pen()

p.penup ()

turtle.bgcolor ("white")
```

(Source: https://docs.python.org/3/library/turtle.html retrieved in March 2021)

These lines of code are no different than those we wrote earlier. They simple determine the color of the background and the pen. However, this information won't be used to draw the main shape because we want to first create smaller shapes that will form the larger shape. This is why we are using the "penup" function once again, so that the pen is lifted right from the start of the program.

The next step is to tell the user to specify how many faces he wants for the spiral shape. To do this we are going to use the "numinput" function once again, and we are going to set a default number of 4 faces in case the user doesn't want to choose. We will also add a limit to this choice by allowing the user to select anywhere between 2 to 6 sides. Let's take a look at some more code:

```
shapeSides = int (turtle.numinput ("Total number of spiral faces", "How many sides do you want from 2 to 6?", 4, 2, 6))

myColor = ["orange", "green", "purple", "blue", "yellow", "red"]
```

Don't forget that the "numinput" function is used to add a title to the window and then ask the question the user needs to answer. In this part of the code we also determined that we want the default value to be 4, then we have a minimum of 2 and a maximum of 6 sides. The user can't ask the program to type a value smaller than 2 or greater than 6 because the program will give him a warning message that the shape can only have 2 to 6 sides. We have also created our list of colors at this stage and we have a maximum of 6 colors to match the maximum of 6 possible sides.

The next step is to define the loop for our object. This will be the main loop and it will place the pen at every corner of the object in order to draw it. Here's how the code looks:

```
for y in range (200):

        p.forward (y * 4)

        location = p.position ()

        direction = p.heading ()
```

This loop is going to take the y variable from 0 to 199 in order to perform 200 passes. Just like before, the pen needs to move forward, but when one corner of the object is reached, the current position of the pen will be memorized, as well as its direction. The position will be measured in x and y coordinates that represent a certain location on your screen. The direction, or the heading as the function is called, represents the way then pen is going. The pen will move in such a way to leave room for the smaller shapes to be also drawn later. That is why we need to memorize these positions and directions, so that the form of the object will be preserved nicely once the program is finished. If we don't tell our application to remember this information, the pen will just go randomly on the entire screen and draw the smaller shapes based on the location of the previous shapes.

The position and the heading commands will be used to gain access to the location and the direction of the pen. The location will be determined based on the x and y coordinates. Remember that x represents the horizontal line and y represents the vertical line. When the two of them intersect, we have a point that will act as the position of our object. The direction, on the other hand, is measured in degrees. It can be anywhere between 0 and 360 degrees. What's important to know here is that 0 translates to up. Based on that information alone, we can imagine the direction of any object before declaring it. All of this data will be stored inside new variables because we need them to determine where to generate the small objects without distorting the large, overall picture. With that in mind, let's now write the inner loop which will draw a shape on every corner of our main object:

```
for z in range (int (y / 2)):

        p.pendown ()

        p.pencolor (myColor [z % shapeSides])
```

```
        p.forward ( 2 * z)

        p.right ( 360 / shapeSides – 2)

        p.penup ()

p.setx (position [0])

p.sety (position [1])

p.setheading (direction)
```

p.left (360 / shapeSides + 2)

File Edit Format Run Options Window Help

```
import turtle
p=turtle.Pen()
p.penup()
turtle.bgcolor("white")
shapeSides= int(turtle.numinput ("Total number of spiral faces", "How many sides do you want from 2 to 6?", 4, 2, 6))
myColor = ["orange", "green", "purple", "blue", "yellow", "red"]
for y in range (200):
    p.forward (y * 4)
    position = p.position()
    direction = p.heading()
    for z in range (int(y/2)):
        p.pendown()
        p.pencolor(myColor [z % shapeSides])
        p.forward(2*z)
        p.right(360/shapeSides-2)
        p.penup()
    p.setx(position[0])
    p.sety(position[1])
    p.setheading(direction)
    p.left (360 / shapeSides + 2)
```

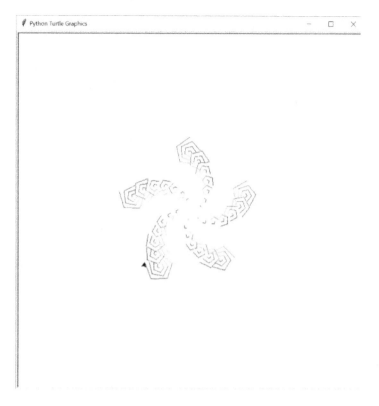

Above is my example with 5 sides:

Let's see what we have so far. Our for loop starts with the variable z being equal to 0 and it ends when its value is equal to half of the y variable, therefore y / 2. The purpose of this operation is to maintain the small objects as smaller shapes than the main object. The structure of these little shapes look exactly the same as the big one, except for the size. In addition, we also tell the program to place the pen down before creating the lines and then lifting it back up after every single line. This way, the main object stays clean without having any interconnected lines.

Next, we set the pen's horizontal position based on the stored position we declared earlier in the code. As already mentioned the horizontal line is called the x axis, therefore to manipulate the horizontal position we need to use the "setx" function. The same thing needs to be done to the vertical position by using the "sety" function instead. Once the positions are clear, we handle the direction which we also stored earlier in the program's memory. Remember that when the main loop ends when 200 passes are reached, we will have 200 small whirly shapes set in a large whirlpool pattern.

That's it, we have finished our new program with the help of nested loops. If you finished your application as well (don't forget to customize it to your heart's desire), you will see that there is a certain disadvantage when working with loops within loops. The main object takes longer to be drawn than the many small objects. This happens because there's a lot more processing going on to create the large shape. The smaller ones don't have that much code that needs to be read and analyzed by the program. All those commands that define the pen and its features, together with all the other functions related to the main object, will make the program take longer to draw the main shape.

Therefore, nested loops can be very handy, but you should know that they will slow down your program. So make sure you don't overuse them, otherwise your system will lag. It might even crash. Nothing may happen when creating such a simple program like this one, but imagine creating a game that has hundreds or thousands of lines of code. Introducing too many nested loops could make that game unplayable. So when you design your program, think a bit about these obstacles because in programming, you always have the option to do the same thing using different methods.

Summary

In this chapter you learned the fundamentals of working with loops. Remember that their main purpose is to turn repeatable code into a loop so that you don't have to write the same steps over and over again. Whenever you need to repeat a set of statements, see whether you can write a loop.

In this chapter you learned about both loop types, namely the for loop and the while loop. When you code your application you need to consider carefully which loop is more appropriate because they work differently. For instance, by using a for loop you can tell the program to execute a number of statements several times. We have used this type of loop in a few of our examples when we had to loop some code 20 times, as long as a variable was within that range. On the other hand, we have the while loop that executes the code as long as a specific condition is still true. This means that the loop can also run until something changes in the program.

This chapter was all about teaching you how loops can modify the way a program runs based on their conditions and the interaction between user and application. In many of our examples we used the "range" function in order to create lists that would later allow us a certain number of times to repeat a set of commands. This controlled the flow of execution. We also used the modulo operator in several cases so that we could loop through a set of list items. This allowed us to modify the colors based on what the user chose from a list of objects. In addition, you also learned that you can create a blank list, which later would be populated with objects or values by using the "append" function. This way, our loops allowed the user to introduce information into our program and then later use it for some other operations.

On top of working with loops, you also learned a number of functions that you can use to extend your programs and make them more interesting. For instance, you learned how to use the "len" function so that you can determine the length of a list. Keep in mind that in this case length doesn't refer to a measurement in inches or anything like that. We are talking about finding out the number of values or items that are inside a list.

In the last section of the chapter you also learned about the concept of nested loops. You created a program using loops inside other loops. You created a main loop that contained a set of instructions, including an inner loop which contained another set of instructions. Using this loop pattern you created a fun looking program that is more complex and interesting than the previous version you created without the use of nested loops.

By going through this entire chapter, you are now able to create for loops in order to repeat any set of commands as many times as you want. You can use the range function to also create lists and limit the number of loop executions. In addition, you know how to create blank lists and then populate them using the append function. Combine the power of the for loops with that of the while loops so that you can execute some instructions only while a specific condition is true. Use all of this information to create new exciting programs either by using these loops on their own, or in combination. You can also create nested loops that contain any combination of for and while loops. Feel free to also write one program using only for loops, and then redesign that program to work with while loops only. This is doable, however, it requires a bit of creativity mixed in with logic because the programs will not have the same syntax. Only by practicing and experimenting on your own you will learn.

Chapter 5:

Conditionals

Computer programs aren't awesome just because they are much faster and more accurate at processing information than humans. They are also capable of making simple decisions on their own. Just think of the many intelligent devices you have around your house or inside a car. Think about the thermostat. Whenever the temperature in your room goes under a certain value, the thermostat will trigger the heating to bring the temperature back up. The same thing happens with most modern security cameras. They won't turn themselves on to start recording until they detect movement. Once the camera's motion detecting sensor is triggered by movement, the camera turns itself on and begins recording. Cars with intelligent braking systems work the same way. Once the car detects an obstacle in front of it, it will initiate the braking system for you in order to avoid an accident. There are many such examples of computerized decision making devices. Other such examples are found in computer games. Just think of any fighting game or roleplaying game you have played recently. Sometimes when your character swings his sword to hit someone, that computer-controlled character will try to block your attack. Decision making processes are part of computers and programmed systems.

In all of the examples above, the computer looks for a number of conditions. Is the temperature in the room too low? Is there someone moving in front of the camera? Is there an obstacle in front of the car? Is the player trying to stab the monster with a sword?

The good news is that you're already a bit familiar with giving your programs the ability to make decisions. In the last chapter we have used the while loop quite a few times. The while loop, also called a statement, is one of the most basic forms of decision making. We need to give the program a condition, and while it is true, the program knows it needs to keep executing the set of commands contained in that loop. But what we want is to give more power to the user, to give him the ability to decide and based on his decision, the program can also decide what to do. For this process, we need the "if" statement.

We are going to start our discussion about decision making with the if statement which we will explore in more detail in the next section. What you should know for now is that it is used to give the program the ability to make a decision based on an answer. If something is true, then the computer will do something. For instance, if the thermostat detects that the temperature is fine in your home, it will decide to not turn on the heating.

In this chapter we will discuss more than just if statements. There are other decision making statements and concepts in Python, such as Booleans, the else statement and the elif statement. We will explore them all, so let's get started!

IF Statements

The "if" statement is one of the most frequently used decision making utilities in any programming language, not just Python. Basically, it lets us tell the system to execute a number of commands based on a certain condition, or multiple conditions. In other words, our computer will be able to make a choice.

The syntax of the if statement is something like this:

if condition:

      type your instructions here

We can have multiple conditions as well, not just one. But for now, keep in mind that the computer tests the statement in the form of a Boolean expression. In other words, it performs a basic true or false test. If the condition is true, then the program will execute all the instructions that are part of the statement. On the other hand, if the condition turns out to be false, the application will simply skip it and execute the rest of the code. Here's a simple example in code this time:

question = input ("Is your name Max?")

if question == 'y':

      print ("Welcome Max!")

print ("ok, have a good day!")

The first line simply asks the user whether his name is Max. Then we have the if statement which says that if the user answers with "y" which stands for "yes", then the "welcome Max!" message will be printed. If the user answers with anything else, this block of code will be ignored and the program will process whatever comes next.

What you should pay attention to in this simple example is the operator we are using. In our if statement we are performing a test to see whether the user's name is Max, therefore we are using an "equal to" operator. However, the equal to operator in this case is not a simple equal sign, but two equal signs instead. The == operator is not the same as the assignment operator because it verifies whether a condition is true or not. It doesn't assign a value to a variable. The test will turn out to be true only if the user hits the 'y' letter on the keyboard. You should also pay attention to the fact that we used single quotes around the letter, instead of double quotation marks. This means that the test is performed to look for that single character and if it appears, then the instructions inside the statement will be executed. If the condition turns out to be true, a message is printed.

In addition, you should notice that the print statement is indented to be part of the if statement. If we do not indent it this way, the program will think that there are no instructions inside the if statement to be executed. If the program doesn't execute this instruction because the condition is false, it will skip all the way to the last line, which isn't indented, and print a different message.

When working with if statements we are also allowed to place loops and even nested loops inside them. All we need to do is indent the loops properly so that Python knows that they are part of the statement.

Now that you have a general idea about using if statements, let's see another decision making conditional statement called the "else" statement.

ELSE Statements

In many cases we want to do something if a condition is true, and something else if it is not true. When working with if statements, if the condition is not true, nothing happens. The program just continues running to the next line of statements. This is why we need to use the "else" statement if we want something to happen when the condition turns out to be false. Just think of a real life situation. You tell your mom to buy you a banana, but you might also consider that the store is out of bananas. So you tell your mom to buy you an orange instead, if they don't have any bananas. The same logic applies here.

Just like with the real world logic about shopping for bananas or oranges, the else statement can only be used after the if statement. We can't write it on its own. That is why in most programming languages it is also referred to as the if / else statement. Here's how the syntax looks:

if this condition is true:

    perform these actions

else:

    perform these other actions

As you can see, the logic behind the else statement is very simple. If the initial condition is true, then the statements inside the if block will be executed and those inside the else block will be ignored. On the other hand, if the condition is false, the if statements will be ignored, and those inside the else block will be executed instead. Now let's take a look at a different type of statement known as the Elif statement.

ELIF Statements

Another option to the if statement is using the elif clause. This is a sort of addon that is used in order to write multiple if / else statements. You will often use these in your applications in order to test for more than just two possibilities. The keyword "elif" means "else if" and is just as logical as the other two statements. Just think about your grades in school. Let's say you get a score of 99 points on your test, so your teacher is going to reward you with an A. But if you get a lower score, the teacher has four other options, not just one other. Using the simple if / else statements, the teacher would only have a choice between A and F, and that wouldn't be a good thing. Fortunately, B, C and D are three other choices, therefore we would have to use several elif statements in order to add these options inside a program.

So, let's work on an example using the grading system. If the score is greater than 95, we will have an A, and all the other statements and test cases will be ignored. If we have a score of 80, it will be a B instead. This means that the program has tested for an A, but the condition wasn't met, so it continued to the next test case, which was for B. This condition was met, so the program continued to ignore the other options. With that being said, let's look at some code!

myScore = eval (input ("Type your test score here: "))

if myScore >= 90:

```
        print: ("you received an A")

elif myScore >= 80:

        print ("you received a B")

elif myScore >= 70:

        print ("you received a C")

elif myScore >= 60:

        print ("you received a D")

else:

        print ("you received an F")
```

Let's break it all down to understand what is happening. First, the program will instruct the user to type in a score as any number ranging from 0 to 100. This number is converted with the help of the "eval" function and then stored inside a score variable called "myScore". The next step is to perform a series of comparisons. First we compare the score that the user typed to a value of 90 or greater. If the user typed a number which is between 90 and 100, the if statement turns out to be true, and the message "you received an A" will be printed to the screen. If the number is smaller than 90, the program continues to the next cases. The program will check to see if the number fulfills the condition of being equal to a B. If it's true, then everything else is ignored. If this condition isn't met either, the program will continue with the next elif clause. If a C is also not true, then the application checks for a D, and if that condition isn't true either, then the else statement will be applied. The else statement works like a final test meant to catch any value that falls out of the values that are true for the other conditions. This means that any number that isn't between 60 and 100 will fall in the else statement.

The if / elif / else structure is often used when creating helpful applications and games because of the many variables that need to be tested. For instance, let's say you are making an app that helps the user decide what clothes to wear. These statements will come in handy because the program needs to check whether it's day or night, summer, winter, spring, or autumn, warm or cold, rainy, snowy or sunny, and so on. So make sure to dedicate enough time to learning all of these statements because you will be using them a lot soon.

Boolean Expressions

Booleans, also known as Boolean expressions or conditional expressions, are one of the most powerful programming tools. These expressions give the system its ability to make its own decisions by evaluating various statements to see if they are true or false. Boolean values can only be labeled as True or False and nothing else. Here's what the syntax looks like: firstExpression conditional operator secondExpression. Take note that these expressions can be nearly anything, such as values, variables, statements and so on.

In one of our past projects we already used a Boolean expression. You might remember it: question == 'y'. Question is the first expression, the double equal sign is the conditional operator, and 'y' is the second expression. The operator we used in this example verifies whether the first expression is equal to the second. Don't forget, one equal assigns a value, so don't use it when comparing Boolean expressions.

With that in mind, there are other conditional operators as well.

Conditional Operators

The most often used operators are the comparison operators and you already used a couple of them before. What you should remember is that these operators are used to check two values and see how they are in relation to each other. Their purpose is to find out if one of the two values is bigger or smaller than the other, or if they are both equal to each other and so on. All of these comparisons will lead to a solid result, which is either True or False. Here's a real world example of such a comparison taking place.

Think about your phone or your computer's login password. When you type the password to gain access to the system, there's a conditional expression that accepts it and then compares it to the correct password. If your password matches the correct one, or in other words it is equal to it, then the expression will return a True value. If True, then you will be allowed into your phone's or your computer's system. Now, let's take a look at the comparison operators in order to learn them.

1. 5 < 10: This translates to 5 being less than 10, which is a true statement.

2. 1 > 3: This translates to 1 being greater than 3, which is a false statement.

3. 4 <= 5: This translates to 4 being less than or equal to 5, which is true.

4. 10 >= 11: This translates to 10 being greater than or equal to 11, which is false.

5. 1 == 2: This translates to 1 being equal to 2, which is a false statement.

6. 3 != 4: This translates to 3 not being equal to 4, which is true.

You may have noticed that some of these operators are not the same as in mathematics. For example, the != (not equal) symbol in Python, is written as ≠ in math. You can't use the math symbol in programming because the language doesn't recognize it as a comparison operator. The main reason for such a change is the fact that the programming version of the operator is much easier and faster to type than the math one.

Another thing you need to pay attention to is that you don't leave a space between the two symbols that make an operator. For instance "==" is good, while "= =" will result in an error because Python reads it as two assignment operators instead of one comparison operator. To refresh your memory:

n = 10

This is an assignment, because we use the equal operator to assign the value of 10 to the n variable. On the other hand:

n == 10

Is an expression which checks to see whether the n variable is equal to 10 and it will either return a True or a False result. To avoid confusing the two operators you should always read the comparison operator as "is equal to". This way, you will memorize the fact that it is a comparison and not an assignment.

Another operator you might have issues remembering is the "not equal to" operator which is made out of an exclamation mark and an equal. You should do the same thing as before whenever you write this operator in your programs. Read it out loud. This way you will easily memorize what != stands for.

Now, as mentioned earlier, the result of using a conditional operator is always a True or False value, which can be the only Boolean values you can get. With that being said, fire up the Python *shell*, and start testing them out. Type any expression you can think of and see what Python gives you as a result. First you will need to declare the variable and assign it a value, however. Only then can you type the second line where you will test whether that value which is now x is equal to a new value. Here's an example:

n = 10

n > 5

True

Since the n variable has the value of 10, when we ask Python to check whether n is greater than 5, it returns "True" as the value, because 10 is a larger number than 5. Go ahead and try out all the conditional operators we just discussed. The process is always the same as in the above example and Python will always return one of the two Booleans, either True or False.

Compound Conditional Statements

When you start planning your own applications and games, you will come across situations where the simple if or elif statements just aren't enough. Sometimes you want to instruct the program to do something if two conditions are true at the same time. For instance, an app that decides for you what to wear might need to test that it's both summer and daylight for it to tell you to wear sunglasses. This is where compound conditional statements come in.

In Python, compound statements are just like in the English language. Here's an example: "I'm going to get dressed and go outside to play." This is a normal compound statement, using the "and" word to say two things. The same way we can perform a test in Python to check whether both of those statements are true. One of the conditions might be false, and then no code will be executed because we need both of them to be true. This is something we do every day, outside of the world of programming. Here are some examples: "If I have a fever and a runny nose, I will stay in bed", "If it's raining or freezing outside, I will wear a thick coat", "If it's not windy, I will wear just a sweater." In these examples, you will notice more than one "operator". When it comes to compound statements we need to pay attention to logical operators. Keep these real life examples in mind while reading about the operators:

1. And: This is the first operator which we used in the first daily life example. In programming, it is written like so: if firstCondition and secondCondition. The instructions that will be written for this compound if statement will only be executed if both conditions are true.

2. Or: This operator is used in the second real world example above and in programming it looks like this: if firstCondition or secondCondition. The result will be true, if any of the two conditions is true. Only one of them has to be true for the code that is part of the if statement to be executed.

3. Not: The last example above shows us how the "not" operator works. Here's the Python syntax for it: If not (condition). The result will be true, only if the condition is false.

By following these rules about the compound statements you can try them for yourself. All you need to do is apply what you already learned about if statements, plus the syntax and rules that come with the compound if statements. If you got this far, you know enough Python programming to slowly start doing things on your own. Don't be anxious, just reread the guidelines and with a touch of creativity you will do just fine.

Summary

In this chapter you learned one of the most important elements of Python programming. You learned how to give a program the ability to make decisions instead of just waiting for a user's command to do something.

We started this chapter by discussing the if statement and how to use it. Remember that this conditional statement works by allows the program to run a collection of instructions when a certain condition is fulfilled. Then we can use the concept of Boolean expressions in order to check for any number of conditions by using the conditional operators, such as greater than or lesser than. In combination with if statements, as well as else statements, we can allow the program to execute a block of code whether a condition is met or not.

Later in the chapter we improved our statements by working with a more complex structure. The if / elif / else statements allowed us to give the program multiple options so that it can make a more elaborate decision. We created a grading using these statements so that the user can find out which mark he or she would receive based on the score received from a test. In this example we gave our program the ability to perform several tests to see which condition is true.

In addition, you also learned about logical operators that allow us to combine any number of statements. You learned how to use the "and", "or", and "not" operators appropriately so that your program can make more difficult decisions.

Now that you know how to use various types of conditional statements, you are ready to start creating more complicated programs and even start making fun games to play with your friends. In the next chapter, we are going to focus purely on the practical side of programming by applying everything you learned so far.

Chapter 6:

Fun Projects and Games

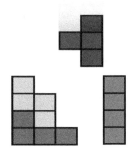

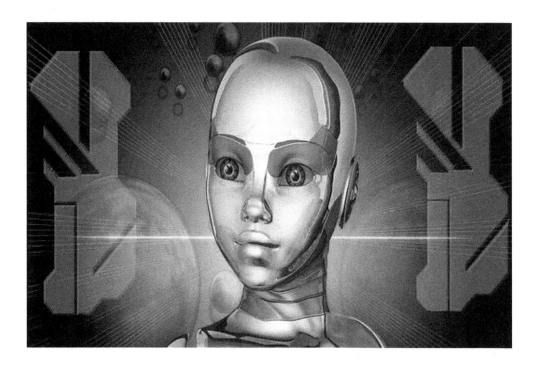

Now that you've finished learning all the fundamentals of programming with Python, it's time to put everything together in application. In this chapter we are going to use almost everything we discussed so far to have some fun and create a few games.

Since games are more interesting when the computer is more directly involved, we are going to rely on conditional statements a lot. After all, games are more fun when the computer is a worthy adversary that tries to beat you. So, before we continue, make sure you fully understand how conditionals work. Practice the other programming concepts as well in order to refresh your memory. Function definitions and mathematical operations will always come in handy when developing a game.

With that in mind, in this chapter we will create a couple of games that rely on chance. We will create Rock Paper Scissors, Pick a Card, and Guess. All three of these games rely on random chance, so the computer will have to choose a random number, or rock paper or scissors. These games are classics, especially nowadays in the world of programming because they allow you to put the basics into practice. We will program the computer to make random choices and decisions and for that we need to plan our games in a smart way. So let's get to it!

Rock Paper Scissors

The first game will be Rock Paper Scissors, which is normally played by two people, but in this case it's going to be you against the computer. The first thing we need to do when creating a game is brainstorming. Take a pen and paper and think about how the game should be designed. Start by first considering the rules of the game, and only then worry about the programming side.

This classic game involves choosing one of three objects, as the name suggests. Once both selections are made, the items are revealed to see who wins. The player who wins is determined by three simple rules. The rock will crush the scissors, while the scissors cut paper and the paper covers rock.

To handle these rules we are going to create a list of choices, similar to the list of colors we created before in some of our drawing programs. Then we will add a random selection function that will represent the choice the computer makes. Next, the human player will have to make his or her choice. Finally, the winner is decided with the help of a number of if statements.

Before we continue with the code, you should start performing these steps on your own. You already have the plan and you know which steps you need to take. So, simply break down the game into easy sections and work on one at a time. If you don't remember how to write an if statement correctly, go back to the chapter about if statements and refresh your memory. The point of this chapter is to help you use what you already know. So give it a try before you read the following code.

Have you tried to create your own version of the game yet? If so, good job! Even if you didn't completely finish it or you wrote the game and you're getting some errors, you should still reward yourself for trying. Now, let's go through the code and see how this game should turn out:

```
import random

selectionChoices = [ "rock", "paper", "scissors"]

print ("Rock beats scissors. Scissors cut paper. Paper covers rock.")

player = input ("Do you want to choose rock, paper, or scissors? (or quit) ?")

while player != "quit":

        player = player.lower ()

        computer = random.choice(selectionChoices)

        print("You selected " +player+ ",and the  computer
selected"+computer+ ".")

        if player == computer:

            print("Draw!")

        elif  player == "rock":

                if computer == "scissors":

                        print ("Victory!")

                else:

                        print("You lose!")
```

```
elif player == "paper":

        if computer == "rock":

                print("Victory!")


        else:

                print("You lose!")

elif player == "scissors":

        if computer == "paper":

                print ("Victory!")
        else:

                print("You lose!")

else:

        print("Something went wrong...")

        print()


    player = input ("Do you want to choose rock, paper, or scissors? (or
quit)?")
```

File Edit Format Run Options Window Help

```
import random
selectionChoices = [ "rock", "paper", "scissors"]
print ("Rock beats scissors. Scissors cut paper. Paper covers rock.")
player = input ("Do you want to choose rock, paper, or scissors? (or quit)?")
while player!="quit":
    player = player.lower ()
    computer=random.choice(selectionChoices)
    print ("You selected"+player+",and the computer selected"+computer+".")
    if player == computer:
        print ("Draw!")
    elif player == "rock":
        if computer == "scissors":
            print ("Victory!")
        else:
            print("You lose!")
    elif    player == "paper":
        if computer == "rock":
            print ("Victory!")
        else:
            print("You lose!")
    elif player   == "scissors":
        if computer == "paper":
            print ("Victory!")
        else:
            print("You lose!")
    else:
        print ("Something went wrong...")
    print()
    player = input ("Do you want to choose rock, paper, or scissors? (or quit)?")
```

Now let's break down the code and discuss each step.

First we import the random package which allows us to use a number of functions that we are going to take advantage of when giving the computer the ability to make random choices. Then we create a list for the three game objects and print the games rules so that the human player knows them. The computer will already know what to do because it is programmed, after all. Next, we ask the player to type his or her choice and then a loop is executed to check the choice of the player. The player also has the option of quitting the prompt window, and when that happens the game is over. Our loop makes sure that if the player doesn't select the quit option, the game will run.

The next step is to ask the computer to select one of the three game objects. This choice is done randomly and the selected item is stored inside a variable called "computer". After the choice is memorized, the testing phase begins to see which player will win. First a check is performed to see whether the two players have chosen the same item. If they did, then the result is a draw and nobody wins. Next, the program verifies whether the player chose rock, and then it looks at the computer to see if it chose scissors. If this is the case, then the rule says rock beats scissors, so the player wins. If the computer didn't select a rock as well, neither did it pick scissors, then it certainly chose paper. In this case the computer will win. Next, we have two elif statements where we perform two more tests that check whether the player selected paper or scissors. Here we also have a statement that checks to see if the player chose something that isn't one of the three possible items. If that is the case, an error message is sent that tells the player he either chose something that he is not allowed, or he mistyped the command.

Lastly, the user is prompted to type the next selection. This is where the main loop goes back to the beginning. In other words, the game starts another round of rock paper scissors.

This game is simple, but it is fun because anyone can win. The computer has a chance of beating you and there's also a real chance of ending up in a draw. Now that you understand how to create a random chance type of game, let's look at other examples to add to our game library while also learning Python programming.

Guess!

This project will be another fun chance based game that will make use of the random module. The purpose of the game will be choosing a number between a minimum and a maximum and then the opponent tries to guess that number. If the player guesses a higher number, he will have to try a smaller one, and the other way around as well. Only a perfect match will turn into a win.

Comparing numbers is something we already did in the previous chapters by using the if statement. We have also used the input function to interact with the program and we are going to make use of it here once again. In addition, we will need a while loop as well.

In this project the random module is needed because of certain specific functions. For instance, we know that we need to generate a random number, therefore we will use a function called "randint" which stands for random integer. The function will have two parameters, which represent the minimum number we can have, as well as the maximum. You can try out this function on its own. Just import the module and then type the following:

import random

random.randint (1, 20)

Python will now automatically generate a random figure between 1 and 20. Keep in mind that the minimum and maximum values are included in the number generation, therefore Python can also generate numbers 1 or 20. You can test this command as many times as you want to make sure that you are truly getting random values. If you execute it often enough, you will see that some values will repeat themselves, and if the range is large enough you might not even encounter certain numbers no matter how many times you run the code. What's interesting about this function though, is that it isn't truly random. This is just a side note that won't affect your program, but it is intriguing nonetheless. The randint function actually follows a specific pattern and the chosen numbers only appear to be random, but they aren't. Python follows a complex algorithm for this pattern instead, and therefore we experience the illusion of randomness. With that being said, let's get back to fun and games. Let's create our game with the following code:

import random

randomNumbers = random.randint (1, 100)

myGuess = int (input ("Try to guess the number. It can be anywhere from 1 to 100:"))

while guess != randomNumbers:

if myGuess > randomNumbers:

print (myGuess, "was larger than the number. Guess again!")

if myGuess < randomNumbers:

print (myGuess, "was smaller than the number. Guess again!")

myGuess = int (input ("Try and guess again! "))

print (myGuess, "you got it right! You won!")

```
import random
randomNumbers=random.randint(1, 100)
myGuess = int (input ("Try to guess the number. It can be anywhere from 1 to 100:"))
while myGuess != randomNumbers:
    if myGuess > randomNumbers:
        print (myGuess, "was larger than the number. Guess again!")
    if myGuess < randomNumbers:
            print (myGuess, "was smaller than the number. Guess again!")
    myGuess = int (input ("Try and guess again!"))
print (myGuess, "you got it right! You won!")
```

That's it! Hopefully you tried to create this game on your own because you already have the tools for the job. Remember that programming is only easy as long as you practice it enough on your own. Just take it one step at a time. With that being said, let's discuss the code in case you need some help figuring the game out:

Just like before, we first need to import the random module so that we can use the random number generating function. Next, we use the randint function with two parameters. As mentioned before, these parameters are the lowest number we can guess, which is 1, and the highest number we can guess, 100. The random number generator will generate a number within this range. Once the number is generated, it is stored inside the "randomNumbers" variable which we declared. This number will not be known by the player because he or she needs to guess it. That's the point of the game.

Next up, the player needs to guess the hidden number. This guess will then be stored inside a new variable called "myGuess". In order to check whether the guess is equal to the number, we are using a while loop with the "not equal to" operator. We do this because if the player gets lucky and guesses the number correctly with the first attempt, the loop simply doesn't finish executing because there's no need.

Next, if the player guesses the wrong number, we have two if statements that check whether the guess is a higher value than the hidden number, or a lower one. An appropriate message is then printed for the player in each case. In either scenario, the player receives another chance to make the right guess. Finally, at the end if the user guessed the number correctly, the program declares victory by printing a message and then the program stops running.

To make the game more interesting you can challenge yourself to modify the random number generator to include different values. You can also add a statement that enables the game to print the score to see how many times the player tried to guess the number. In addition, since the game ends when the player guesses, you could write a main loop so that the player can choose to restart the game instead of automatically quitting. Have fun and don't be afraid to try anything.

Choose a Card

Card games are always fun and they also rely on random elements to some degree. No matter the card game, chances are quite small to have multiple identical games. This means you won't get bored any time soon. With what we discussed so far about Python programming, we can create a card game. It might not look good, unless you have an artistic friend to draw everything for you, but you could still create the graphics with the help of the Turtle module like we did for other projects. This will require some patience though. In any case, we can create a card game even without graphics by simply generating the name of each card. Instead of seeing a virtual card, we will see the name "four of spades", or "queen of hearts".

Before we continue, you should take note that this project is your challenge. You have learned everything you need to write such a game, and we already created two other fairly similar projects. So this time, you are almost entirely on your own. As usual, start with a pen and paper and figure everything out logically. Worry about the code afterwards. However, to help you out a little, we are going to brainstorm together just to give you some ideas.

One of the simplest card games we could create involves a game with two players that battle each other to see who draws the card with the highest value. Each player will randomly pull a card from the deck, and the one who has the higher card will win. It is a simple game, but fun due to the random element.

Since we won't be using any graphics, we will have to create our deck of cards some other way. We are going to set them all up as a list of strings since we will be using their names instead. Next, we need to give the players the ability to randomly pull a card from the deck. This means that we are going to use the random module once again and we will add a choice function that randomly distributes cards to the players. Finally, we need a way to compare the two cards that are drawn by the two players. As you probably guessed, this is a case for comparison operators.

That is pretty much all it takes to create a card game. You can add more features, or remove some if you aren't interested in them. Whatever you do, design the game on paper so that you know your goals. Then work one those goals one line of code at a time. This way you will write your game in no time and whatever problems you encounter you will be able to fix fairly quickly.

Quiz ? ☺

Let's test your knowledge about loops, conditionals, operators and more! Try your best to answer the questions and then go to the Answer Key chapter to check the results.

1. What is iteration?

A program test.

A decision.

The repetition of certain steps.

2. Which statements will use iteration?

if and while

for and while

if and else

3. Is the following statement true?

The while loop will iterate until told otherwise.

True

False

4. Which symbol is translated as "equal to" in Python?

=

!=

==

5. Is the statement 5 >= 5 true?

Yes.

No.

6. Which loop is used to repeat a statement a specific number of times?

indentation

for loop

while loop

7. Which data type can only be true or false?

integer

boolean

float

8. Which symbol needs to be placed at the end of a conditional statement?

;

:

...

9. Is the following statement correct?

Repeat loops will repeat if the condition is true.

True

False

10. Which symbol means greater than or equal to?

\>\>

=\>

\>=

Summary

In this chapter you have taken everything you have learned so far and used it in practice to create a couple of fun games. Nothing improves learning better than using games to study. You have successfully designed and coded three random chance-based games using conditional statements, loops, and with a little help from the random module. Hopefully, you have tried to create these games on your own because you learn best by trying, even if you end up failing. That is why we also discussed the first two games together, code included.

The third game, however, is left for you as a sort of a final challenge. You have the basic idea behind the game and what needs to be done to write it. All it takes is a bit of persistence and creativity. So have fun developing games as much as you have fun playing them!

Chapter 7:

Glossary

When learning a programming language, or just programming in general, you cannot help but come across many terms that you don't understand. A lot of these terms aren't used in our daily vocabulary, or they have a completely different meaning in the world of programming. Therefore, in this glossary you will find the most important terms that are used throughout this book.

Algorithm

A collection of instructions that are used to achieve a goal. Imagine a number of ingredients for a recipe.

Append

Introducing something to the end of something. For instance, adding items to the end of a list.

Argument

Passing a value to a function. Sometimes called a parameter.

Boolean

An expression that can only be true or false.

Concatenate

Combining two strings to form just one.

Conditional expression

A statement that gives the program its ability to check a certain value and then perform a set of actions based on it.

Expression

A collection of variables, values, functions, and operators that lead to a result.

For loop

A type of statement in programming languages that repeats a section of code based on a range of values.

Function

A collection of statements that can be reused to perform various actions.

Import

Bringing a block of reusable code, or a set of functions inside any program in order to have access to its functionality.

Index

The position of an element inside a list.

Initialize

Assigning the first value to a variable, or any other item, in other words, giving it its initial value.

Input

Entering data into a program or a system. An input can come from a keyboard, mouse or any other device that can record information. These devices are also called input devices.

List

A collection of items or values.

Loop

A collection of commands that the program will repeat a certain number of times.

Module

A type of file that contains various functions, classes and variables that can be used in any program once imported.

Parameter

A variable that is attached to a function within its definition.

Range

A collection of values found between a minimum and a maximum value.

Shell

A command line user interface that reads and executes your commands directly. IDLE is an example of a *shell*.

String

A character sequence that can form words or sentences. They include letters, symbols, numbers, as well as spaces.

Syntax

The programming structure or rules of a certain coding element. In a way, it is the grammar of programming.

Variable

A value with a name, which can always change inside the program.

While loop

A statement that repeats a collection of instructions while a certain condition is true.

Chapter 8:

Answer Key ☑

Here are the answers to the quiz from Chapter 3 that checks whether you know the basics:

1. print

2. NameError:: name"f" is not defined

3. Defines a function that doesn't do anything.

4. 6

5. Orange

6. True

7. Type Error

8. Error / Name Error

9. False

10. 0

Here are the answers to the quiz from Chapter 6:

1. Repetition of certain steps.

2. for and while

3. True

4. ==

5. Yes

6. for loop

7. boolean

8. :

9. False

10. >=

Conclusion

You have made it to the end and have learned a great deal about programming in Python, as well as programming in general. When you started out you probably didn't even know if programming was a topic that is suited for you, but if you made it this far, it means that you are at least curious about it and capable enough to become a coder yourself.

With the help of this book you learned all the basics of Python programming. Take note that this means you also learned the basics of programming in general, because the main concepts that appear in Python are also valid for other languages such as C, C++, Java, and so on.

With that being said, let's briefly summarize what you've learned thus far:

1. You started from the very basics, learning how to download and install Python. You probably don't even remember anymore how it felt to start from nothing.

2. The first real concept you learned was that of variables. You explored different types of variables such as numbers, strings, and lists.

3. Next up, you progressed towards functions. You learned how to make your code reusable to avoid writing tedious amounts of code. Always remember that functions are one of the fundamental building blocks in programming.

4. In the fourth chapter, you spiced up your knowledge of programming with loops. You learned how for loops and while loops are used to make more complex programs, as well as nested loops.

5. Then you progressed to using conditional statements to make your programs more intelligent. Statements like If and Else will be used in all of your programs because of how versatile they are.

6. Finally, you have created several games using all this knowledge you gathered through the course of this book.

When you summarize everything like this, you might be thinking that you didn't learn that much. That couldn't be further from the truth. In fact, you learned about the majority of concepts and techniques that are used in programming.

From here onwards, all you will do is polish your skills and introduce new ideas that will improve the ones you just learned. So make sure to practice everything you just learned and you will become a good programmer without a doubt. Even if you struggled with some concepts, just break them down into simpler elements. If you still find yourself in need of help, join one of the countless online programming communities that are absolutely beginner friendly. Learn with others and above all, have fun because this is a journey to learning a skill of the future.

Thank you for reading this book and learning the basics of programming. The world always needs more programmers and developers. If you find that the book was helpful and that you have learned a great deal from it, make sure to leave a review.

References

Chun, W. (2007). *Core Python programming*. Upper Saddle River, NJ: Prentice Hall.

Lutz, M. (2018). *Learning Python*. Beijing: OReilly.

Paz, A. R. de, & Howse, J. (2015). *Python game programming by example: a pragmatic guide for developing your own games with Python*. Birmingham: Packt Publishing.

Romano, F. (2015). *Learning Python: learn to code like a professional with Python - an open source, versatile, and powerful programming language*. Birmingham: Packt Publishing.

BOOK #2: UP to EXPERT CODING

LEARN Python
Up to Expert Coding

Dominique ◆ SAGE

Introduction

Python continues to amaze the world of programming, data science, machine learning, and AI development with its efficiency and versatility. Not so long ago, you made the choice to become a part of this world and continue improving your skills by carrying on with your journey to mastering Python up to the expert level.

This book is the continuation of *Learn Python: Kids & Beginners*, so it's recommended for you to go through that one first unless you already know the basics. The purpose of this book is to help you learn the more difficult concepts such as formatting, object-oriented programming, working with external files and JSON data, and extending your horizons with Python libraries and modules.

My name is Dominique Sage, I have been programming and developing applications and games in the industry for almost 20 years. I'm now investing my time to share my knowledge with you. This book is meant to guide you step by step with enough theory and practical examples to get you started in the real world. Join me and learn how to unlock the real power of Python!

### Chapter 1:

Mastering Python Building Blocks

In the previous book, we explored all the basic elements that are used in Python programming. You learned how to use them individually, creating very simple programs. Now, it's time to learn how to unlock their power and versatility and use them together to solve complex problems.

In this chapter, we are going to dig deeper into Python programming and learn how to calculate numbers using functions, explore mathematical functions, and deal with time zones. You'll also learn about classes and objects, which are essential elements to day to day programming no matter the language you're using. Finally, you'll enter the world of massive data and learn the power of dictionaries.

This chapter builds upon the fundamentals you learned from the previous book in the series. Before getting started you should refresh your memory about integers, floats, strings, loops, and lists, because we'll be using them a lot in order to learn more complex topics. Are you ready? Let's get started!

Numbers, Strings, and Dates

Computers and programming languages don't process information the same way we do. It's all about numbers, whether they are floats, integers or Boolean values. The computer needs to perform a number of calculations behind the scenes in order to interpret data and accomplish a certain task. At the same time, text is stored in the form of character strings and mathematical operations can be performed on them, too.

All of this can be understood by a computer because it operates based on numbers and calculations. But what about dates and time zones? Computers don't care about this human concept without which our society and economy cannot function. Take note that by default Python doesn't recognize date and time because there's no datatype to represent these values. However, there is a module that understands this type of information. We just need to import it. We'll get to that soon, but first, let's talk more about numbers, functions, and mathematical operations.

Using Functions to Calculate Numbers

If you recall, functions allow you to pass something to them so they can give you a result. For instance, programming languages like Python have functions that work just like those you learned when you first started using a calculator back in school. Look at the square root function that's on any calculator. It is a function because you declare a number and in return you receive the square root of it. In case you don't recall from our previous lessons, a function can be described with the following formula:

myVariable = myFunction (parameter, [parameter])

Since nearly every function returns a value, we should first define a variable to store that value. Then we have a number of parameters, also known as arguments, inside parentheses, where we pass at least one value. For instance, if we have an absolute function, or abs(), it will require one value in order to return a new value. And just in case you're rusty at math, if we use this function to pass a positive number, we will receive that exact same number as the final value. However, if we pass a negative number, then we'll obtain the positive version of it. Here's an example of this in Python code:

a = -10

b = abs (a)

print (a)

print (b)

We have two variables, a and b. Variable a has a preset value, while variable b is assigned the absolute value of variable a. This is why we use the absolute function. If we print the first variable, nothing changes. But, if we print the second variable, the result is the absolute value of a, which is 10. This is a simple example to get you back on track with functions. This one in particular only returns a single value, but other functions aren't so restricted and can return more.

Python comes with a series of built-in functions, such as:

1. float(x): Convert an integer or a string into a float.

2. round (x, y): Round the value of x to y number of decimal points.

3. max (x, y, z, a, b, c, ...): Return the largest value from the declared parameters.

4. min (x, y, z, a, b, c, ...): Return the smallest value from the declared parameters.

5. bin (x): Return a string value that represents x as a binary value.

These are just some of the built-in Python functions. Use the help command to learn about more functions or just Google the entire list by typing "Python built-in functions". Don't forget about your previous lesson on functions, because you can use these basic functions to create nested functions.

However, the aforementioned functions may be useful sometimes, but they're often not enough. There are many situations where you'll need more complex math functions in order to deal with a problem. This is especially true if you're interested in data science or machine learning where some heavy math is required. Fortunately, there are many Python libraries and modules out there that expand the language's usability, and you can easily download and import them.

Math Functions

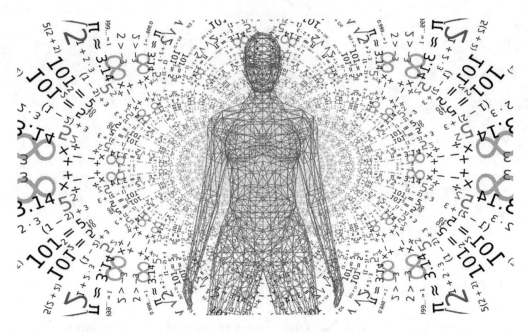

Whether you're using a simple command prompt, the Jupyter development environment (check it out, it's great!), or your favorite Python file editor, you can import the math module by typing "import math". This loads the module and makes a number of mathematical functions available to you. On a related note, other modules can be imported the same way, so if you're interested in how you can extend Python in the future, search for the list of Python modules. It is quite extensive and diversified, and many of them are used in fields like data science and machine learning.

One of the functions you'll have access to is the square root function we mentioned earlier. This isn't part of basic Python, but after importing the module, you can now try the following example:

import math

print (sqrt (36))

Oops! You get an error. But why? We imported the math module, didn't we? Yes, we did, but the problem is we still wrote the function the same way we would declare normal, built-in functions. When using module functions, we need to also include the name of the module, followed by a dot and then add the function. Here's how:

import math

x = 36

print (math.sqrt (36))

6.0

Now we have the result of the function, which is 6.0.

The math module we imported adds a great deal of functions, including trigonometric, logarithmic, and hyperbolic functions, as well as constants such pi. We're not going to explore all of them because learning mathematics is beyond the scope of this book, especially because only certain fields require advanced notions beyond the standard operations you learned in the previous book. But if you're interested nonetheless and you have some math knowledge, you can play around with the following functions:

1. math.cos (x): This will return the cosine of x radians.

2. math.degrees(x): This function translates the angle of x from radians to degrees.

3. math.e: The value of e is a constant equal to 2.7182…and it doesn't require parentheses. The same goes for pi, which is another constant. These are exceptions to the rule.

4. math.log (x, y): Return the natural logarithm of x to base y.

5. math.factorial (x): This will return the factorial value of x.

There are a lot more functions included in the math module. If you plan to pursue a path in data science or machine learning, you should look them up and brush up on your skills in mathematics.

So far you learned how to use integers and floats, but we never explored the idea of formatting. What do you do when you have to work with sums of money and a specific currency? How do you force Python to display a comma to separate thousand places? For instance, we don't want Python to list our price values with precise decimal calculations. We want something like $2,2042.50 instead of 22042.5004356324256. All of this and more can be achieved with the help of f-strings.

Formatting with f-strings is fast and easy. We simply need to insert an "f" followed by some information in between quotation marks. Here's a simple example:

f'Hi {myUser}"

The "f" character instructs Python that everything that comes after is a format string. This means that what we have in the quotation marks is the literal section of the code that we want to be displayed as it is. What follows inside the curly braces is the expression, which is a placeholder for the result that appears once the code is executed. In between these braces we can only have a variable, a calculation formula, or both options combined. Here's another example in code:

myUser = "Bob" print (f'hi {myUser}")

The result of this code will be the word "Hi" with a space after it and followed by the information contained in the "myUser" variable. Now let's take a look at an example with numbers where we'll have a formula as an expression:

itemPrice = 25.49

myQuantity = 100

print (f'Subtotal: ${myQuantity * itemPrice}")

The result looks like this: $2549.0.

This works, but it's not perfect for real world application because it's not the way we like to look at dollar amounts. The sum is missing a comma that would make the amount easier to read, and we like to see the pennies declared as two digits no matter what. We want the dollar amount in our example to look like this: $2,549.00.

F-strings are perfect for this and in order to achieve our desired formatting, we need to use the format string inside the braces of an expression inside the f-string. This means that the f-string will begin with a colon that will be inserted in the closing curly brace, next to the variable or value that will be displayed. In order to add the comma as well, we'll need to place it inside the format string, next to the colon. Here's how it will look in code:

print (f'Subtotal: ${myQuantity * itemPrice:,}")

Now the result should be $2,549.0. But we still don't have the two penny digits we want. The solution is simple. After the comma, we need to insert ".2f" which stands for "fixed two decimals". This means that Python is instructed to never display more or fewer than two decimals. Let's add this to our code:

print (f'Subtotal: ${myQuantity * itemPrice:,.2f}")

And here's our result: $2,549.00.

That's it! We have achieved the formatting we were looking for. Whenever you need to make a program that displays numbers with appropriate comma separators and a specific number of decimals, just use format strings. They are simple to use, effective, and they allow you a lot of freedom.

Numbers Are Sometimes Strange

As someone just entering the world of programming, you're probably used to using simple numbers. So far you didn't have to use imaginary numbers, or any other numbers that aren't in the base of 10. After all, calculating sums of money or creating a Snake game clone doesn't require the use of weird numbers found only in your math class. However, if you're interested in advancing at some point beyond programming and entering the world of data science, you'll need to know about these strange numbers. So let's start by learning about some of them, like the octal, binary, and hex numbers.

If you need to use numbers in the base 2, 8 or 16, Python contains the symbols needed to write the functions that include these types of numbers. Here's an overview where you'll see the used digits, symbols, and functions:

1. Binary: This is a base 2 number represented by the "0b" symbol and the "bin()" function.

2. Octal: This is a base 8 number represented by the "0o" symbol and the "oct()" function.

3. Hex: Also known as hexadecimal, this is a base 16 number represented by the "0x" symbol and the "hex()" function.

If you're already feeling a bit intimidated, don't worry. As mentioned, if you've never even heard of these numbers before, you probably won't be using them any time soon either. Most programmers and developers never have to deal with them. So if you think this is a bit too much, you can skip this section or just go through it to get the general idea. Maybe someday this knowledge will help you.

Now, if you're also getting your hands dirty with some fancy computer science exercises, you'll need certain functions to translate one number system to another. Numerical conversion can be done easily in Python, even in a console. Here's an example of converting the number 342 into its hexadecimal equivalent:

print (hex (342))

The result will be 0x156. The "0x" symbol is mentioned in order to note that this number, 156, is a hexadecimal number. Now, in order to convert numbers backwards, from hex or binary to decimal, we don't have to add any function. All we need is the print statement with the hexadecimal number inside the parentheses. Here's an example:

print (0x156)

The result is our initial decimal number 342.

Next up we have the so-called "complex numbers". This is another category of strange number that you'll probably never use unless you're really into high mathematics and engineering. But hey, it's always good to know them in case you have an electrical engineering buddy that won't shut up about his work.

Complex numbers are those that are expressed using the "a + bi" formula, where a and b represent the real numbers and i represents the imaginary numbers that follow the $x^2 = -1$ equation. This equation is the reason we call these numbers imaginary. There's no such scenario where squared x is equal to -1. Lost yet? No problem, because Python adds a bit more confusion by marking imaginary numbers with a "j" instead of "i" like they're expressed in mathematics. In any case, if you ever write an application using complex numbers, you need to create this imaginary number. In order to do so we need to use the "complex()" function. Here's how it looks:

complex (realNumber, imaginaryNumber)

In code this would be:

x = complex (2, -3)

Our x variable will receive 2-3j as the imaginary number. If we want to display this number we'll just print the variable. However, we can also attach ".real" and ".imag" to the variable in order to print just the real part or the imaginary one. Here's an example:

print (x.real)

The result is 2, which is the real number part of the variable.

These are just the basics to give you an idea, but if you don't fully understand because math isn't your strong point, don't worry about it. Working with so-called "weird numbers" isn't a must in order to learn and master Python programming. You just need to know that Python has all the tools you need if you ever have to use complex numbers or other types. In addition, if you think you'll be working with these numbers, you can import the cmath module and learn more about such functions.

Methods and Strings

Methods are just functions that are attached to a certain object. In Python, all strings are in fact string objects or str objects. The second version is the more accurate one because in Python 3 str replaces the old string version. So, to avoid confusion, remember that the string object is the old version of the str object, which is also pronounced like string object. Yup, that's probably still confusing, so just remember that in Python 3 str just refers to any string of characters. With that being said, a str method is a bit different from a function. Here's how the syntax looks:

string.myMethod (parameters)

In this formula, the string is the character string we're working with. Next, we have a method that can be applied to the string and it's followed by a set of optional parameters that are passed to the method. Here are a few methods that you can use on strings in order to change them or their behavior:

1. capitalize(): The string in question will be returned with a capitalized first letter, while the rest will be lowercase.

2. lower(): All characters in the string will be returned in lowercase.

3. upper(): All characters in the string will be returned in uppercase.

4. title(): Each word in the string is returned with a capitalized first letter.

5. swapcase(): This method switches lowercase letters to uppercase and the other way around.

6. istitle(): This method will check whether the string contains letters and whether the first letter of every word is uppercase. It returns a True or False result.

7. count(a, [b, c]): This method will return the number of times the "a" string is found inside our initial string to which we attach this method. In addition, we can insert "b" and "c" as the two limits that define the part of the string we want to analyze.

Use what you learned about string in the previous book together with these methods and play around. There's no need to memorize them. Just practice with these and Google others by typing "string methods" whenever you need them. Programming often involves more researching skills than memorization techniques.

Dates and Times

Dates and times are used in a lot of applications, like those designed for scheduling or financial planning. Just think of all those times you get a notification about a Windows update, a scheduled Steam update, or any other online application you use. Timestamps are also often used in order to register a user's actions or the occurrence of an event. Finding reasons to work with dates and times in Python isn't the problem because they're plentiful in every tech field. However, for some strange reason Python doesn't offer us a built-in data type to represent these data structures the same way it does for integers and character strings.

In order to play with dates and times we need to import a module. The module in question is aptly named datetime. As usual, at the beginning of your application or at the start of prompt you'll type "import datetime" in order to gain access to the features provided by the module.

This type of module is known as an abstract base class, which means that it introduces new data types to a programming language, in this case Python. Here are some of those data types that you'll be using most often:

1. datetime.date: This is just the date without time, so we'll be able to manipulate only the day, month, and year.

2. datetime.time: This is the data type that's strictly about time, which is expressed in hours, minutes, seconds, and microseconds. In addition, it allows us to access time zones.

3. datetime.datetime: This data type includes all of the above.

Now, let's start with the first one, the "date" data type. We're going to use this one when we don't need to know anything about time. So let's see how we can create an object that contains only date information. We have two options. We either use the "today()" method, or we also declare the year, month, and day. The first option will take data from our computer's internal clock and therefore will use the current date. The second option allows us to add a custom date. Just make sure to declare the year, month, and day in that particular order.

The first rule you need to remember is that you can't use zero as a first digit when declaring the day and month. In other words, a date like "2020,01,01" isn't going to work. Instead you need to write the date like so: 2020,1,1. Now let's see some actual examples:

today = datetime.date.today()

lastDecade = datetime.date (2019,12,31)

Don't forget to import the datetime module before writing the code. In this example, we simply store the present date in a variable called "today". Afterwards, we store a new date in a second variable called "lastDecade". Next, we can use a print function to see what each variable contains. Just keep in mind that your "today" variable won't display the same data as in this example because it's based on the present date. In addition, we can learn or use only a part of the date by specifying it. Here's how:

print (lastDecade.month)

print (lastDecade.day)

print (lastDecade.year)

As a result, the month, day, and year will be displayed separately.

We discussed earlier that the default date format is year, month, and day. However, it can be formatted using the f-strings we played around with in the last section. Another option involves using "strftime" to format time and date, but even though it's a solid method, we're going to stick to f-strings because they're newer and more future-proof.

When working with f-strings, remember to place all symbols and spaces in the proper order you want them to appear in the end result. Let's take a look at an example:

print(f"{lastDecade:%A, %B %d, %Y}")

The result will be: Tuesday, December 31, 2019

If you want to just use the date but in a different format, like month / day / year, then change the f-string like so:

today = f"{today:%m/%d/%Y}"

The result will look like this: 04/08/2020. Yours will be a different date because we're using the present date.

You might be asking yourself what's up with those strange symbols. They are called directives and are used when creating datetime formatting strings. Here are a few examples:

1. %A: Displays the full name of a weekday, such as "Tuesday".

2. %a: Same as the above, but it displays the abbreviation of the name. In our example it would be "Tue".

3. %B: Displays the full name of the month. Use the %b directive if you're looking for the abbreviation.

4. %Z: Displays the time zone, such as EST.

5. %c: Displays the date and time in the local format.

There are quite a few more and we'll go through some of them in later examples. If you want to explore them now, just search for "dates and times f-strings directives" or something along those lines.

Now, if you're developing or even just using an online application, your computer should be set to display the accurate date and time based on your location. When connected to the Internet, the web extracts that internal data from the Network News Transfer Protocol. This protocol takes time zones and even daylight savings time in consideration.

If you don't need to work with dates, however, you should use the time class. Let's look at the syntax and then create a time object. Again, don't forget to import the datetime module if you haven't already. The syntax is simple and logical:

myVariable = datetime.time ([hour,[minute,[second,[microsecond]]]])

Take note that the parameters are optional. You don't have to use any of them, in fact. Here's a scenario where you'd actually want that:

midnight = datetime.time()

print (midnight)

The result is 00:00:00.

In most cases you'd stick to using hours, minutes, and seconds. You can also use format strings once again in order to change the format to suit your needs.

Depending on your project, you might need to use only dates or times. However, in most real world scenarios you'll need to record an accurate time and date of an action that's taking place. This is where you'd use the datetime class. Here's an example by using it with the "now" method to extract and display the date and time as shown on your computer:

import datetime

presentTime = datetime.datetime.now()

print (presentTime)

The date and time depends on when you run the code, but it should look like this:

2020-04-08 12:43:22.345456

You may notice that a line of our code is a bit awkward looking, namely the datetime.datetime part. That's because we're declaring the datetime class which is part of the datetime module, and both of them have the same name. To change that, we can import the module and give it any descriptive nickname we want. Here's how that works:

import datetime as dt

Now you can type "dt.datetime" instead and not repeat yourself in confusing ways.

How to Deal with Timespans

We often need more than just the date and time when developing apps or games. It's not enough to know the current time or date; we need the timespan, also referred to as duration. Python's datetime module contains the class we need and it's called timedelta.

In Python, whenever we want to calculate the timespan between two dates or times, the timedelta object is automatically generated. Let's say we want to set up a few variables: one for the last day of the year, and one for the Easter holidays. Then we need a final variable that will be placed in the result we obtain from subtracting an older date from a newer date. Here's how this would look in code:

import datetime

newYear = datetime.date(2020, 1, 1)

memorialDay = datetime.date (2020, 5, 25)

daysTimespan = memorialDay - newYear

You'll notice that we'll get the timespan as the total number of days between the two periods, plus the "00:00:00" time because we didn't mention any times for the two dates. By default, the time will be set to zero. In addition, the timedelta object is created automatically because of the timespan calculation we just made. However, we can declare a timespan, or timedelta, by following this structure:

datetime.timedelta (days =, seconds =, microseconds =, milliseconds =, minutes =, hours =, weeks =)

If we don't mention any parameter values, they will be set to 0 by default. Otherwise, we need to include them after the equals sign. Let's take a look at an example to see this in action. We are going to declare a date, generate a timedelta by using the timedelta class, and then obtain a new date by adding the timedelta and the initial date together.

import datetime

newYear = datetime.date (2020, 1, 1)

myTimespan = datetime.timedelta (days = 146)

print (newYear + myTimespan)

You can also calculate a subtraction or play with datetimes. Let's say we only need the timespan that is shorter than a day and it's printed in time and date:

import datetime

myStart = datetime.datetime (2020, 4, 25, 7, 0, 0)

myFinish = datetime.datetime (2020, 4, 25, 15, 35, 0)

myTimespan = myFinish - myStart

print (type (myTimespan)

Result: 8:35:00 <class 'datetime.timedelta'>

We obtain the duration between the two dates and times, but we also introduced something new, "type ()", which allows us to print the type of the data type we use. That is how we can confirm that we have generated a timedelta, which represents a time span, instead of a date or o'clock time.

Keep in mind that we don't always need to measure time down to the microsecond, or even second. For instance, when we need to figure out someone's age, we declare two dates. One is for the birth date and one for the present date. In this case, we don't need to calculate the timespan with such extreme precision. Let's look at the example:

import datetime

presentDay = datetime.date.today()

birthDate = datetime.date (1990, 12, 3)

myAge = (presentDay - birthDate)

print (myAge)

What we'll get is the timespan measured in days, followed by the default 0:00:00 time. But this isn't what we want. After all, we measure age in years, not in days or weeks. So, we need to convert the timedelta to the number days by adding ".days" to it. We'll add this to a new variable, which will be an integer. This is important because with integers, we can perform simple mathematical calculations. Let's look at the example:

myAge = (presentDay - birthDate)

myDays = myAge.days

print (myDays, type (myDays))

The result is still measured in days, but now it's an integer instead of a timedelta type class. Now we can perform a simple division by the number of days in a year. Take note that if we're purely interested in the years, we should use the floor division operation "//" and not the standard division. In case you're not familiar with this operator, you should know that it's used to return a number without any decimal points. In addition, if we have a negative number it's going to be rounded away from zero, or in other words it will be floored, but that's not the case here.

myYears = myDays // 365

print (myYears)

If you also need the number of months, you can use the same operation by dividing the remainder of the previous floor division by 30, which is the number of days in an average month. Don't forget that to get the value of the remainder you'd have to use the "%" operator.

Time Zones

As you probably know, just because it's morning where you live doesn't mean it's morning everywhere in the world. The globe is divided in time zones and depending where you're located, the time and day will differ from other places. We do have something that's called universal time, or Universal Time Coordinated to be exact (UTC). There's also Greenwich Mean Time (GMT) which is often used, but both follow the same idea. The planet's prime meridian, the middle of the time zone, serves as the center of the time zone map (0) and the further away you go from this point, the higher the time offset will be.

So why are we talking about time zones in programming? Time zones matter when dealing with datetime information because Python provides us with two separate datetime types. The first is referred to as the naive datetime because it doesn't involve time zone-specific data, and the second is called the aware datetime because it includes that information.

By default, the date, time, and datetime objects we created are naive. However, timedeltas and the dates defined using ".date" are naive no matter what. We can only include time zone data inside the datetime and time objects.

Take note that when you request the current time from your computer's internal clock, it will be in your local time zone, but it's not specified. This is where you can try to use the .now function and compare the result from it with the .utc_now function. The second one gives you the UTC time for your location. By comparing the two results, you can make a subtraction and see the difference. For instance, it might be 12 pm where you live, but it's 7 pm UTC time. That means that your time zone is UTC -7 hours.

Time zones can sometimes be tricky, but here's an easy way to tell the difference by looking at the time zone map. Everything on the left side from the center is the East and that's where the sun rises no matter the time zone. So, if you already saw the sun rise in your area, that means it already rose everywhere to the right on the map, but not the left.

If you need to use different time zones, you'll most likely need to import "gettz", which stands for "get timezone". This function is part of the "tz" class that belongs to dateutil. So, you need to specify the component exactly when importing it. Here's how:

import datetime

from dateutil.tz import gettz

This is how you import a specific item inside a class or a module without importing everything.

Now we can use the gettz ('time zone name') syntax in order to access the time zone we need. Just replace "time zone name" in the parentheses with the name of the time zone. In order to do that, however, we can't use any time zone name we want. Instead, we need to use the names found in the Olson database (also known as the tz database, tzdata, IANA, and zoneinfo). This database uses a simple naming convention and contains all the data we need for each time zone and location. For instance, if we need US Eastern Time, we will type "America/New_York" in the gettz declaration. If we want central European time, we'll type "Europe/Paris". Google the database if you need other time zones because they are quite a few and there's no need to memorize them. Now, let's take a look at an example where we'll use five time zones:

```
import datetime

from dateutil.tz import gettz

# Current UTC time.

utc = datetime.datetime.now (gettz ('Etc/UTC'))

print (f' {utc: %A %D %I : %M %p %Z}")

# Current US Eastern time.

est = datetime.datetime.now (gettz ('America/New_York'))

print (f' {est: %A %D %I : %M %p %Z}")

# Current US Central time.

cst = datetime.datetime.now (gettz ('America/Chicago'))

print (f' {cst: %A %D %I : %M %p %Z}")

# Current US Mountain time.

mst = datetime.datetime.now (gettz ('America/Boise'))
```

```
print (f' {mst: %A %D %I : %M %p %Z}")

pst = datetime.datetime.now (gettz ('America/Los_Angeles'))

print (f' {pst: %A %D %I : %M %p %Z}")
```

As you can see, it's quite simple. Just don't forget about those handy format strings that make reading the result so much easier. It might not be the most exciting code you've ever written, but you never know when you'll be writing an app that needs to extract time zone information.

Summary

In this chapter, you warmed up by using what you learned in the previous book in order to advance further. Functions, strings, formatting, and dealing with time are all core parts of Python programming and you'll encounter them a lot. As you can see in all of our examples, formatting with f-strings and their versatile directives can help us read any data a lot easier. High math functions might not help you if you're not into data science, but knowing how to make your data more readable will. Furthermore, numbers, strings, and time are all basic components. This chapter's purpose was to simply show you that you can do a lot more with them and that they aren't just a beginner's building blocks.

Chapter 2:

Using Dictionaries to Deal with Massive

Data

Python dictionaries are similar to the lists we discussed in the previous book. The main difference between them is that list items are identified through their position, but dictionaries are identified by a unique key. The key can be defined by us either through a number or a string. The only thing that matters is that the key has to be unique for every single dictionary item.

Uniqueness is important. To get a better idea about how all of this works, just think about ID numbers, phone numbers, and account usernames. If more than one person had the same username, they would all have control over the account and their notifications. If more than one person had the same ID or social security number, then imagine the chaos if one of them had a serious debt.

The key is equal to something unique that later can be linked to a certain value. This value can be anything: a string, number, list, or any other data type. To get a better picture of a dictionary, just imagine a table that has a column that contains a unique item, and a second column that contains data attached to that first column. Here's how that would look:

Key	Value
"jsmith" =	"John Smith"
"nadams" =	"Nick Adams"
"fbaggins" =	"Frodo Baggins"

In this example, we have the left column containing name abbreviations. In case you're wondering, something like this can be used by a company to generate and keep track of user accounts given to their employees. However, the value doesn't have to be a name, or a string to be more specific. It can also be a number or a list. Here's another example where we associate a value that contains the name, hiring year, a number that can represent anything we want, and a Boolean value that can be used to tell us which employee received a company car and who hasn't.

Key	Value
"jsmith" =	["John Smith", 2015, 3, True]
"nadams" =	["Nick Adams", 2018, 4, False]
"fbaggins" =	["Frodo Baggins", 2006, 5, True]

Dictionaries can also contain a number of keys that represent only a fragment of the data, not all of it. For instance, instead of having a unique key assigned to a row dedicated to every item, we can create a dictionary for every employee. Afterwards we can designate a unique key to each bit of data. Here's how such a dictionary might look for the first employee listed in our previous examples:

"jsmith" =	"name" =	"John Smith"
	"year_of_employment" =	2015
		3
	"team_size" =	True
	"has_company_car" =	

The next employee can have the same dictionary key names, such as "name" and "year_of_employment", but the values attached to those key names will be different. Having dictionaries with multiple keys is easy when programming in Python because the language allows us to access any item we want. The syntax is simple. All we need to do is follow the "item.key" rule. Here's how:

jsmith.name = "John Smith"

jsmith.year_of_employment = 2015

jsmith.team_size = 3

jsmith.has_company_car = True

Using the name of the key in order to access whatever we need is a lot easier than working with indexes. Using the position of an item isn't very descriptive and when we have a lot of objects to deal with, we might get lost pretty quickly. Here's how the code above would look using an index just for the sake of reference:

jsmith[0] = "John Smith"

jsmith[1] = 2015

jsmith[2] = 3

jsmith[3] = True

As you can see, the previous example has more information for us as programmers and it makes the code more readable. You decide what's best for you because both options work just as well.

Now that you have some basic knowledge about data dictionaries, let's learn how to actually build one.

How to Create a Dictionary

The syntax for creating a dictionary is simple. Let's analyze it:

myName = {key:value, key:value, key:value, key:value, ...}

In this example, "myName" is anything we want and it describes the subject to what the key/value pairs refer. Take note that the pairs need to be inside curly braces and they don't necessarily have to be strings. They are sometimes used as integers as well, but rarely anything else. What's important is to separate the key from the value which we assign to it by using a colon. The value can then be anything we want, as discussed earlier. Finally, we can have as many key/value pairs as we need. Just don't forget to place commas as separators. Finally, we can make the syntax easier to read by writing each pair in its own line. This way if we have a dictionary with a lot of items, we can easily revisit them without getting lost in a seemingly endless line of key/value pairs. Nothing really changes about the syntax however, so the code would turn into something like this:

myName = {

    key:value,

    key:value,

    key:value,

    key:value,

...

}

Now replace the syntax with actual keys and values like we discussed at the beginning of the chapter. In the next section, we are going to learn how to access the data so that we can manipulate it.

Gaining Access to Data

Once you created the data dictionary and added in the values, we can work with them in more than one way. The easiest thing we can use is the print function for the entire dictionary when we need to display it. Here's an example using the data from our first dictionary:

print (employees)

{'jsmith': 'John Smith', 'nadams': 'Nick Adams', 'fbaggins': 'Frodo Baggins'}

However, in real world situations, you would rarely do this because normally we need to access a specific object, not the entire dictionary. In order to do that, we have the following syntax:

myDictionary [key]

In other words, we declare the name of the dictionary we're interested in and then specify the key we're looking for. Let's say we want the value associated with the "nadams" key. Here's what we would type:

print (employees ['nadams'])

Python will now return the value or values associated with the 'nadams' employee. As you can see, nadams is bound in between quotation marks because it's a string. Alternatively, we can declare a variable, store the string inside the variable and then call it instead of calling the string directly. So, let's create a new variable and call it "juniorProgrammer". Next, we are going to print the dictionary item by calling "juniorProgrammer", a variable, instead of the "nadams" string which will be inside that variable.

juniorProgrammer = 'nadams'

print (employees [juniorProgrammer])

Another useful command we'll often use when playing with dictionary data is the "len" statement. Sometimes we need to learn the length of a dictionary and the easiest way to do that is using the len function the same way we use it when working with lists. Here's the syntax:

len (myDictionary)

In programming, length usually refers to the total number of elements inside something like a list, dictionary, or tuple. Here's an example where we set up a dictionary and then add the length of it to a variable called "numberOfEmployees".

employees = {'jsmith': 'John Smith', 'nadams': 'Nick Adams', 'fbaggins': 'Frodo Baggins'}

numberOfEmployees = len (employees)

#display the number

print (numberOfEmployees)

The result in this case will be 3 because that's how many key/value pairs we have inside the dictionary. On a side note, dictionaries can also be empty and therefore have a length of zero.

Next, we might want to check whether a specific key exists. We can search for it using the "in" keyword, and the verification process will return a True or False result. In the following example we're going to look for two keys, one that we already know exists and another that doesn't. Let's see how it all turns out:

employees = {'jsmith': 'John Smith', 'nadams': 'Nick Adams', 'fbaggins': 'Frodo Baggins'}

Does the dictionary contain a jsmith?

print ('jsmith' in employees)

Does the dictionary contain a bpop?

print ('bpop' in employees)

Output:

True

False

As you can see, the print function together with the "in" keyword tells us that the first key exists and the second doesn't.

The problem with this method is that when you search for something and it doesn't exist, there's a chance the application will crash. We don't want that. So to make sure that can't happen, we should use the "get()" method that works like this:

myDictionary.get (key)

Take note that in this case we are no longer using square brackets, but we're back to using parentheses. So, in order to search for something in our dictionary we should type something like this:

juniorProgrammer = 'jadams'

print (employees.get (juniorProgrammer))

The difference between using the get method and any other is that your program won't crash once a dictionary item can't be found. Instead, you'll see a "None" result and the program will continue executing everything else that comes after. You can also pass a second value to the method so that it returns something else when a failed return occurs. In the next example, we are going to look for a key that doesn't exist, but instead of printing the default word "none" as a result, it will return a different message. Let's see how it works:

print (employees.get ('bepop', 'No clue what you're talking about'))

Now you'll see a custom message when the "bpop" element isn't found and your program won't crash.

Next, we have another key aspect of dictionaries (pun not intended), which is the fact that they are mutable. This means we can use code to change what they contain. Here's the syntax for this procedure:

myDictionary [key] = myValue

As usual, replace "myDictionary" with the name of your dictionary, as well as the key and the value. For instance, let's say that John Smith who's an employee just changed his name to John Smith-Grey, so the company he works for will have to update his record. In this case we wouldn't want to delete all the previous information and recreate it. We just need to keep the key we used earlier and make modifications to the value. All we would have to do is change the following line:

employees ['jsmith'] = "John Smith-Grey"

Now if we follow up with a print statement, we'll see that the new value has been added.

Keep in mind that in the real world, dictionary data is most likely stored permanently on an external file. This would make our code insufficient and we'd have to write more code to change that file so that it can save the new information. We won't dive into that since you're just getting introduced to working with dictionaries, but it's something to be aware of for the future.

Changing Data

You can make changes to the data stored in a dictionary by using the "update" method. This is the standard way of inserting new items or modifying values. Let's take a look at the syntax:

mydictionary.update (myKey, myValue)

Take note that if the new key you're trying to insert already exists, nothing will happen. The new key has to be unique in order to be added. As for the value, the new one will replace the old one through the update. Let's analyze an example where we have an "employees" dictionary and try to insert two new names into it. We'll start from scratch, building the dictionary:

employees = { 'hsolo': 'Han Solo', 'wadama': 'William Adama'}

Next, we will update the value of the second key:

employees.update ({'wadama': 'Bill Adama'})

print (employees)

Next, we will use the update method to introduce a new key/value pair to the dictionary:

employees.update ({'hpotter': 'Harry Potter'})

Let's see the results. The first update modified the value of "wadama" from William Adama to Bill Adama. The previous name was changed, because the key we specified was found in our dictionary. As for the second update, our dictionary didn't have an "hpotter" key. This means that the update method didn't have a value to modify with the one we declared. Instead, the update created and added a new key/value pair to our dictionary with the name we specified.

From this example, we can conclude that our code doesn't specifically mention whether we're looking to change a value or add a new one in. Isn't that a problem? The answer is no. There's no need to make the difference because Python does it automatically. As we already know, keys are unique. We can't have multiple rows using an identical key. This means that whenever the update is performed, there are two checks it goes through. First, it tries finding an identical key. If it already exists, then only the value of that key will be updated and nothing else will be added. The second check revolves around the key not existing in our dictionary. If there's no key, there's no value to update, therefore a new key will be created with the name you specified. This decision making process is performed automatically without us even knowing it because it's simple.

Once our previous code is processed, we will have a dictionary with three objects, including the one with the modified value. Now let's type the following code to see everything our dictionary contains:

for person in employees.keys():

print (person + "=" + employees [person])

Now the program will display everything in our dictionary, both the keys and their values.

As you probably already thought, we can loop through dictionaries as well, just like we do through lists. However, doing so in the case of dictionaries provides us with a few more options.

The first thing we can do is loop through every object inside our dictionary with the help of a "for" loop. This way we can extract all keys inside.

for person in employees:

print (person)

Next, we might want to access all the values in the dictionary. All we need to do is change the print statement and keep the same for loop.

for person in employees:

print (employees [person])

On a side note, we can do the same thing by changing the fol loop slightly by introducing the ".values" method and attaching it to the "employees" dictionary in the for loop statement.

for person in employees.values ():

print (person)

In addition, we can loop through both keys and values all at once. All we need is the ".items" method to be added to the dictionary inside the loop. However, we will have to introduce two variables after the loop. One will work as a reference for the key, the other for the value. We can access both types of information by using the names within the print statement's parentheses. Here's how this works:

for key, value in employees.items ():

print (key, "=", value)

In this example, we use the key and value variables. They can be anything we want. You can name them differently. They are used to loop through employees.items and the print will provide us with the key and the value during each loop cycle. Take note that for the sake of readability we also added an equal sign in the parentheses so that we can keep the key separate from the value.

Now, the next question is how do we copy or delete dictionary data? Before deleting, however, we probably want to copy the dictionary data first, just in case. So, let's take a look at the syntax:

myNewDictionary = myDictionary.copy()

Using our previous dictionary as an example, we can see that both of them are the same when printing the information they contain.

As for deleting data, we have more than one option. First, we can use the "del" command in order to delete any item by using its key. Here's how:

del myDictionary [key]

In the following example we are going to create a new dictionary and then use the delete function to remove all items that are attached to a specific key. Then we'll print the dictionary to make sure those objects were removed.

#Defining the dictionary

department = {'jrprogrammer': 'Junior Programmer', 'srprogrammer': 'Senior Programmer', 'dbmanager': 'Database Manager'}

Display dictionary

print (department)

Delete dbmanager

del department ["dbmanager"]

Display the contents of the dictionary again.

print (department)

That's it! The item attached to 'dbmanager' has been removed from our dictionary. Now, keep in mind that if you don't specify a key when using the delete function you will remove the entire dictionary from your program. So if you type "del department", you'll no longer have a dictionary to work with and when printing its contents you'll see an error. Something that no longer exists cannot be displayed. However, if you need to delete the key/value pairs but keep the dictionary, you need to use the clear method instead of the delete method. It looks like this:

myDictionary.clear()

In the next example, we are going to recreate the same dictionary we used above and then print it. Afterwards we're going to use the "clear" method to remove all the information without deleting the dictionary itself.

department = {'jrprogrammer': 'Junior Programmer', 'srprogrammer': 'Senior Programmer', 'dbmanager': 'Database Manager'}

```
print (department)
```

Remove the information inside the dictionary.

```
department.clear ()
```

```
print (department)
```

Now the result of the print is just two empty curly braces. In Python language this means that you still have a dictionary, but it doesn't contain anything.

Summary

Dictionaries are an important part of Python programming because they help us manage massive data. Always remember that simplicity is key and overcomplicating things when creating an application is just going to lead to an overcomplicated mess in which even you as the original programmer will get lost. That's why dictionaries should be used to simplify things, even though they may seem a bit more confusing than lists, for instance. In this chapter you learned the core of what makes a dictionary. Now you know how to create one, how to loop through its items, and how to perform a number of operations using several dictionary methods.

Chapter 3:

The Power of Classes

In the previous book, we talked a lot about functions and since then we've used them often because they allow us to manage blocks of code for particular tasks. In this chapter, however, you will learn about the concept of classes, which also allow you to manage blocks of code but they are far more powerful. You will explore the many aspects of classes and learn how to work with objects. They are the main component of all object oriented programming languages, including Python. They are essential to any real world programming task that involves more than a simple tic tac toe game. So, let's get started and enter the world of serious programming.

Object Oriented Programming

Object oriented programming, usually known as OOP, is a concept that's been floating around for at least two decades. Its name refers to the fact that it implies a model similar to real life objects. These objects, just like in the real world, have certain characteristics or attributes that make them special. For instance, your desk is an object. But we have a huge number of different desks in the world. They are not created equal because they differ in design, size, color, type of material, features, and other things. The only common aspect is the fact that they're all desks.

Or think about cars instead. We all know what a car looks like, but they aren't all identical. They're defined by various attributes like brand, type, model, year, color, fuel type, horsepower, engine type, and so on. In addition to attributes, they are also characterized by a number of "methods" that are shared, such as start, go, turn left, turn right, break, and stop. All of these actions are taken by all cars no matter their attributes.

In the two examples, the chairs and the cars are classes. The class creates them all in all their forms and variations. Once the class builds a car, it becomes its own independent object. If we change this particular car's attributes, the class itself will not be affected. Other cars won't be affected either.

You can think of classes as a schematic or pattern that is used to create a number of objects. If you don't like our previous examples, think of cats instead. Sure, we don't have a cat factory that's building them after a blueprint, but there's DNA which works kind of like a schematic used to create different cats. Cats come in different colors and sizes, but they have the same behavior no matter what. This behavior can be considered to be methods, like purring, eating, and sleeping. Even we humans are objects in the same way.

When you write your code, you can create a class that will manage every member that belongs to it. These members will have unique attributes, like name, birth date, and username. There should also be a number of methods that will control the accounts created by people. For instance, we should have a ".restore" method for a forgotten password, or ".delete" to remove an inactive account. Methods provide us with control. The basic idea is that the instances of one class are in fact objects we use for various tasks. We can manipulate them and change them as needed without affecting the class or other members.

This is the concept of object oriented programming, hence the name. It's one of the most important concepts you'll learn as a programmer because no job interview in the field goes without mentioning it. Most modern programming languages, including Python, are object oriented languages used to develop serious software as well as complex games. So, let's summarize the most important terms you need to know when learning this type of programming:

1. Class: They are blocks of code used to create an object, which becomes an instance of that class. Imagine our schematic scenarios discussed above.

2. Instance: A section of data created from the class. This is what's also known as an object, where each instance is a different object spawned by the class.

3. Attributes: Objects, or instances of a class, have certain characteristics that describe them. In programming, attributes are sometimes also called properties.

4. Methods: Classes often have functions attached to them, which define what actions they can perform. For instance, a car class would have a "go" method, which is attached to the name of the class (or object) with the use of a dot. Like so: car.go.

Now, let's create our own class and focus more on instances and attributes.

How to Create a Class

Classes are created the same as functions. You can name them however you want as long as the name begins with a letter and contains no punctuation marks or spaces. However, when it comes to classes, there's an unwritten rule generally agreed upon by programmers around the world. The name of a class should start with an uppercase letter. Yes, you can use lowercase letters as well, but by using an uppercase letter we are able to quickly see the difference between a class and any other variable. You'll read a lot of code, and following such rules and conventions will make it much easier. So, to begin, you need to type the keyword "class", followed by the name you give it and a colon. Here it is in code:

class Dog:

Don't forget that you can also use comments to make your code more readable and understandable.

Next, we need to create objects, also called instances. In order to do that we need to first enable the class to have that ability, and to do that we use the "init" method, which stands for "initialize". Since this is a typical method, it works just like a function, but it's defined within the class. The only difference is that the method is declared with two underlines before and after, like so:

__init__

You might hear other programmers refer to this is a dunder init, which simply means a double underline initialization. So, let's take a look at the syntax for this method:

def __init__(self [, prop1, prop2, prop3, ...])

The first keyword is "def", which stands for "define", followed by the initialization method. Now, our class can create instances. Next, we have the "self" keyword, which is just the name of a variable and it points at the instances we're creating. Take note that you can use any other variable name, but in this specific case the word "self" is used as an industry standard because of its self explanatory nature.

Now, let's go through a simple example to see how a basic class is created and defined. We are going to create a class called "Subscriber" and inside it we're going to pass a username and a full name in order to create a subscriber any time needed.

Define the class to be able to create objects.

class Subscriber:

def __init__(self, username, fullname):

Once the initialization is performed, we end up with an instance, or object, called "self". This object is currently empty. What we have so far are two parameters called username and fullname. They will contain the data we'll pass into them later. Having an empty instance doesn't help us with much, so we'll need to introduce the information that makes it relevant and unique. So the next stage we need to assign a value to all of the instance's attributes (we'll talk more about those soon).

Once we defined the class, we're going to create the instance with the following syntax:

myObjectName = Subscriber ('username', 'fullname')

Instead of "myObjectName" we'll have the name of our instance, and the two parameters will be replaced with an actual username and full name that will be attached to the newly created object. Take note that you shouldn't indent this code. If you do, Python will see the new lines as part of the class when it shouldn't be. What we want is a way to verify the class. So let's set up a new subscriber with a username and full name.

myFirstSub = Subscriber ('Bob', 'Bobby Jackson')

If the program executes this line without an error, we know it works. But we should test it by printing the instance. Therefore, to verify the data inside the instance we created we should print the entire thing. Keep in mind you can also print just the attributes, or parameters. Here's how it works:

print (myFirstSub)

print (myFirstSub.username)

print (myFirstSub.fullname)

print (type (myFirstSub))

Once each line is executed, you'll see a series of results. The first output looks something like this:

<__main__.Subscrriber object at 0x000002175EA2E160>

This line tells us that "myFirstSub" is an instance that was generated using the Subscriber class. If you're wondering about that number at the end, don't worry about it, it's just a reference for the object's location inside the memory. Next, we have the other three lines that look like this:

Bob

Bobby Jackson

The first line is the username, followed by the second line which is the full name. Finally, we have the type, which shows us that our instance is an object that belongs to the Subscriber class. This concludes the class test.

Before we continue, take note once again that when we say object or instance we're talking about the same thing. In programming, both words are synonymous. The same thing goes for attributes and properties, such as the username and full name we used. They're one and the same concept and we'll talk more specifically about them soon. For now, just remember that objects are used to store blocks of data on something that is similar to something else (all cats are just cats, no matter how different). The object's uniqueness is then defined by attributes or properties. Attribute names should be descriptive and clear. That is why we used "username" for instance, instead of shortening it to something else that could cause confusion.

Attributes

Now that we've defined a class and we have an empty object, we can actually take its attributes and add data into them. By data we mean values, of course. For instance, let's assume that we need all of our objects to have a username and a full name attribute that stores each user's username that is needed to log into an online account. Here's how we write the definition for those attributes:

self.username = username

self.fullname = fullname

In the first line we create the attribute called "username" and place inside it some information that will be used when we make a call to the class. The second line does the same thing. Let's see the whole code, with the class, to get a better view of the bigger picture:

Defining the Subscriber class.

class Subscriber

def __init__(self, username, fullname):

Defining the attributes and adding the values.

self.username = username

self.fullname = fullname

To summarize, first we create the empty object. Next, we introduce the username attribute and associate it with the object. Then we place inside the attribute the value that is passed in as "username". We do the same thing for the second attribute, "fullname". All of this is also made clear by following a clear naming convention.

Once we have the object, we can also make modifications to the values attached to the attributes with the help of this syntax:

myObject.myAttribute = myValue

Replace each element with the appropriate names you used. Here's an example:

newSubscriber.username = "Arthas11"

If you test your code again, you'll see that the username has been changed to the new one we just added, while the full name stayed the same.

Take note that you don't always need to pass a value to each attribute. However, if you know that you'll always have the same value when an object is generated, then you can use the following syntax:

self.myAttribute = myValue

The value can be anything: a Boolean value, a date, the result of a calculation, anything you want.

For instance, when we generate a new object, we might want to also keep a record of when it was created. So, we're going to add a new attribute called "dateCreated". We'll probably also need the ability to enable or disable a user's account, so we'll also add an attribute called "isActive". However, this also means we'll have to set a default value for a newly created username/account, so we need to set the new object to True, which is a Boolean value. In order to achieve all of this, you'll have to import the datetime module and remember everything we talked about in the first chapter. Make sure you add the import command at the beginning of the program, at the top of the class definition line. Next, we can start writing the new attributes and declare their values:

self.dateCreated = dt.date.today()

self.isActive = True

Did you manage? If you forgot how, no problem. We're going to take a look at the entire code in case you're struggling:

```
import datetime as dt

# Defining our subscriber class.

class Member:

def __init__(self, username, fullname):

# Defining the attributes and assigning the values.

self.username = username

self.fullname = fullname

# Default date when the user account was created is set to today's date.

self.dateCreated = dt.date.today()

# By default, the user account is set to active.

self.isActive = True
```

Remember that if you don't import the datetime module at the beginning of the program, you'll see an error when you execute the code that tells you the "dt.date.today" line is unknown. Furthermore, we don't have to introduce any more information inside the class for the two new attributes because we can define them through code whenever we want. As for the default value we created, it just means that it will be assigned whenever we generate a new class instance without having to declare anything else. However, in programming, that doesn't mean we can't change it. We can always make modifications to a default value the same way we change any attribute's values. For instance, let's say that the "isActive" attribute decides if the user is allowed to log into his or her account. If a user breaks the rules of your application or website, you'd no longer want to allow him that privilege. This means that we need to change the default value of True to False. Here's how:

```
newSubscriber.isActive = False
```

That's it! As you can see, the rules and the syntax stayed the same even though we're dealing with a so-called default value.

Class Methods

All class objects you create can have as many attributes as you want and you can name them however you like. Just think of our previous car and cats examples. In addition, you can also create your own methods for those objects. The main difference between the attributes and the methods is that methods refer to the behavior of the object, not just static information such as color and size. So, while a cat's attribute can be the color, its method, or behavior, would be its ability to eat, sleep, or purr.

Methods are in fact not much different from the basic function you learned about in the beginner's guide. The only real difference between the two is the fact that a method is connected to a class and the objects that derive from it. The name of a method is also different from that of an attribute because we use parentheses after the method, in which we can declare a set of parameters. Here's how the syntax looks:

def mymethod (self[, param1, param2, param3, ...])

The syntax is self-explanatory, but keep in mind the parameters are optional. Therefore, you shouldn't use the square brackets at all, unless you need to pass some parameters after "self".

Now, let's define a new method called "display_date_created". On a side note, remember that we can use the underscore symbol to act as a sort of separator between words inside the names of methods or variables. Since we want our methods to be clear and easy to read, you might prefer this naming convention. It's up to you. Now let's take a look at the code that defined our new method:

def display_date_created(self):

return f"{self.fullname} joined on {self.datecreated:%m/%d/%y}"

If you recall what we learned earlier, you'll see that the purpose of this method is to compile some text that is neatly formatted using an f string. The text will contain the name of the subscriber and the date when the user was created. Just keep in mind that the method will fulfill its task only when it's called. So, let's take a look at the syntax for the method call:

myobject.mymethod()

Replace the placeholders with the appropriate names and don't forget the parentheses. They're a must even if you don't pass any parameters inside them. Parameters are used to pass information into methods the exact same way they do into functions. However, the difference here is that we always need to have the "self" part first. Let's see an example. We need to define an "activate" method in order to check and see if a subscriber can log into his account. So, we need to set the access to True if he can or False if he can't. Here's how we can do that:

def activate(self, yesno):

self.is_active = yesno

When we execute this method, we won't see anything because it simply modifies the attribute "is_active" for a specific subscriber to anything that's passed inside the "yesno" parameter.

Remember that methods are just functions connected to a certain class. The methods we worked with so far are referred to as instance methods because we tied them only to objects, which are instances of the class we defined. However, in Python we can also have class methods.

Class methods apply to the whole class and not just certain objects created from it. This means that we won't have to use the "self" keyword anymore because we don't need to refer only to a specific instance. "Self" can't be used as a reference to an entire class. So, the first thing we need to consider when defining the class method is avoiding using the "def name (self)" definition completely. However, excluding this from the definition isn't enough unfortunately. A class method starts with the following line:

@myclassmethod

The "@" symbol tells us that this is a so-called decorator. While this sounds strange, it's another programming term you have to get used to. Decorators are elements that modify the functionality of something to which they're attached. After the decorator, we can type the following line:

def mymethod(cls,x):

Change the "mymethod" placeholder to whatever method name you want, but leave the "cls" part. That's used as a reference to the entirety of the class because the decorator defined it that way in the background. After "cls" we can introduce any parameters we need to apply to the method, just like before.

Now, let's say we need to create a method that determines a number of days before certain objects are created. This means that every instance deriving from our class will have the same number of days. How can we accomplish this? We'll start by defining a class variable called "clear_days" that will have a default value equal to zero:

```
@classmethod

def setcleardays (cls,days):

cls.clear_days = days
```

These lines provide Python with the instructions to set the value of "clear_days" whenever the "secleardays" method is called. Let's see a full example to get a better idea of what's going on:

```
import datetime

class Subscriber:

clear_days = 365

def __init__(self, username, fullname):

self.datecreated = datetime.date.today()

self.trial_expired = datetime.date.today () + datetime.timedelta (days = Subscriber.clear_days)

@classmethod

def setcleardays (cls, days):

clas.clear_days = days
```

Now when we execute this code, we'll have the "Subscriber.secleardays(30)" line which calls to the "setcleardays" method inside the class to pass the value of 30 into it. This means that within our class, the initial "clear_days =0" variable will now accept the value of 30 instead. Now if we add the following block of code to our program, we'll create a subscriber and the program will tell us the date it was created and when it's going to expire:

john = Subscriber ('jsmith', 'John Smith')

print (john.date_created)

print (john.trial_expired)

Keep in mind the result depends on when you execute the code. The initial date will be whatever today's date is. As for the "date_expired", it will be 30 days from today, or any other value we specify instead of 30 inside the "Subscriber.setcleardays()" line.

These are more or less the basics of dealing with classes and methods. But we aren't quite done yet. In the following section we're going to discuss another type of method, namely the static method.

Static Methods

Static methods will begin with the "@staticmethod" decorator. However, what makes this type of method different from the above is the fact that we don't have to attach it to a certain object or class. Static methods are in the truest sense functions that are defined part of a class. In fact, the only reason to use a static method is to maintain clean code and organize your project in such a way to easily read it and modify it at a later date.

In any case, static methods are defined the same way as the other methods, except we're not going to use self and cls because they're not bound to a certain instance or class. At least, not in the same sense as the typical class methods. Now, let's see an example to clear up some of the confusion:

@staticmethod

def presenttime():

rightnow = datetime.datetime.now()

```
return f"{now:%I:%M %p}"
```

As you can see, we created a familiar method called "presenttime", but we don't attach it to any object or class, and we don't pass any information into it either. Its only purpose is to give us the present datetime in the format we specified in the last line of code.

The Concept of Inheritance

When we talk about object oriented programming, we can't avoid paying attention to the concept of inheritance. In fact, this is the heart of the matter. OOP is all about class inheritance and subclasses, so let's dig a little deeper into the rabbit hole.

At the beginning of the chapter we mentioned cars, cats, and schematics. We described the classes as schematics, or plans, used to build objects as members of that class. To recap, remember that while all cats are unique in some way, they are still cats because they are all objects that are part of a family (class). So, each cat that's unique inherits certain characteristics from its class. The key word here is "inherit".

The concepts of inheritances, classes and subclasses didn't just come out of nowhere to make our lives harder. Thanks to them, we can store and categorize the world's entire data by breaking it into neat classes, subclasses, and unique objects. For instance, think of other animals we sometimes call cats, but they aren't cats. Think of lions, panthers and pumas. They're felines, just like cats. They inherit some of the same behaviors and characteristics found in the cat class. And we don't need to stop here. After all, all cats are felines, which in turn are mammals. Therefore, they inherit certain characteristics that are found in all mammals. Then we can go further and say that all mammals are animals and they inherit some attributes from the animal class. So, everything that makes a cat what it is, is the sum of all the characteristics inherited from the many other classes that come before it. Inheritance starts at the top from the most general category and it goes all the way down to the unique object.

You can also apply this analogy to cars as well. Just picture vehicles as the master class from which automobiles, boats, and airplanes inherit some of their characteristics. Then let's choose automobiles, under which we have personal cars, buses, vans, trucks and so on. Then we can take cars and see all the different manufacturers like Ford and Nissan. We can go on and on until we get to the very specific car that we have in mind.

In programming, the most common method of using the concept of inheritance is by creating a number of subclasses inside a parent class. The parent class will define everything that may apply to the child classes (subclasses). In turn, the child class will define only what matters to the subclass, but without making changes to the characteristics it inherited.

The Parent (Main) Class

What inheritance means is that all child classes will inherit the attributes and methods from their parent classes. On a side note, you might hear about parent classes being called main classes or base classes. The same goes for child classes being called subclasses. Don't let the names confuse you.

The parent class is basically no different than any other class we talked about in our previous examples. All classes follow the same rules. So, we're going to use our Subscriber class once more, but we won't use some of the data we added to it earlier. Here's how we'll stick to the basics:

import datetime

class Subscriber:

#All subscriber accounts will expire within a year since creation.

expires_in = 365

#Class object definition

def __init__ (self, firstname, lastname):

#Characteristics that are valid for all subscriber objects

self.firstname = firstname

self.lastname = lastname

#Calculating when an account will expire from today

self.expiration_date = datetime.date.today() + datetime.timedelta (days = self.expires_in)

We have set all subscriber accounts to expire after a year since they've been registered. Therefore, the purpose of this class is to define the variable "expires_in" to a value of 365. This value is later used in our application to calculate the exact date of expiration. In a future example you'll see that we'll be able to use this variable with a different value from within a child class. For the sake of simplicity, in our example we only used two parameters. You can try out this code by creating a subscriber and printing his first name, last name, and subscription expiration date:

Will = Subscriber ('Will', 'Riker')

print (Will.firstname)

print (Will.lastname)

print (Will.expiration_date)

The result is the subscriber's first name, last name and the date, which should be one year from the moment you run the code.

In the real world, however, we would have different types of subscribers. Let's say there would be Plus subscribers and Premium. Both categories will share the characteristics provided by the parent class. Therefore, when we define them as child classes of Subscriber, they will inherit the parent class' methods and attributes.

The Child Class

In order to define a child class (subclass) we need to write it outside of the main class with the following syntax:

class childclass (parentclass):

Replace the placeholder names with whatever you want. Here's an example creating two subclasses called Plus and Premium, which will be the child classes of Subscriber:

```
class Plus (Subscriber):
```

```
class Premium (Subscriber):
```

Right now, we can't test these subclasses because they don't contain any data. We'd receive an error. Since you won't always want to fill in the class with information as soon as you declare it and save it for later, you can use the keyword "pass" right after each class definition. This instructs Python to allow the classes to pass without an error message even though they contain nothing. You can also add a comment before them to remind you what their purpose is:

```
# Child class for Plus subscribers.
```

```
class Plus (Subscriber):
```

```
pass
```

```
# Child class for Premium subscribers.
```

```
class Premium (Subscriber):
```

```
pass
```

Whenever you need to use the child classes, you can do so without referring to the main class. Both the Plus and Premium subclasses we created will inherit everything from their parent class automatically. So, let's take an example by creating a Plus subscriber called Patrick. The syntax will look like this:

```
Patty = Plus ('Patrick', 'Morisson')
```

Now, do the same for the Premium subscriber:

```
Bob = Premium ('Robert', 'Idaho')
```

Next, we can test the code like we did before using print statements to check what data is found inside the accounts we just created. Take the example we used earlier with subscriber Will and go through the test yourself. You'll see that both subscribers will automatically have the same attributes from the parent class.

Child classes will accept any parameter that the parent class can accept. They are assigned to attributes, the same way they were for the Subscriber class. However, in the case of the two child classes we created, they are just class instances that don't have anything unique about them. Normally, child classes would have something different about them and not just inherit the characteristics from the class they derive. One of the easiest things we can do with these child classes is assign an attribute that is set to a default value within the main class, but has a different value when used by the subclass.

For instance, let's say that next to the Plus and Premium subscriber classes we also have a Lifetime Member subclass. In this case we wouldn't want to have an expiration date for the account, so we need to set it accordingly. To do that, we just need to set the "expiration_date" inside the new "Lifetime_Member" subclass and delete the "pass" part of the code because we're going to add a new line. Here's how it would all look in code:

```
class Life_Time (Subscriber):

#Make the subscription expire after an absurd amount of time, like 200 years.

expiration_date = 365.2422 * 200
```

Any value you use in the subclass will automatically override the one that is set to be the default inside the parent class. Keep being creative with classes and subclasses until you get the hang of them.

Summary

Classes, including child classes, are often used in any programming language, including Python. With what you've learned so far, you should be able to create your own classes and subclasses. Eventually, you'll want to use classes whenever possible, especially as your program or game becomes more and more complex. For now you can survive with simple functions, but you should get into the habit of working with classes.

In programming, you should never be afraid to take one step back in order to take two steps forward. Even if you start off using functions and basic data types at some point, you'll realize that you're lost in all of the mess you created. Too many lines of code, too many repeating blocks, and way too many variables can overwhelm you quickly. This is another reason why classes are so useful. They allow you to cut out all the repetition and confusing gibberish by bringing order. So, when you feel your code is bloated, take a break, go back, and look where you can replace blocks of code with classes and subclasses. As you progress, all you'll have to do is make a call to them, or create a new subclass instead of rewriting an entire block of code.

Chapter 4:

Cleaning Your Code

All we can ask for is a smooth running program with no errors slowing us down, but sometimes the dice just rolls against us. It might be something we overlooked, like a simple spelling error or syntax error, or it might be something that happened to the program with no fault of our own. No matter the case, it's our job as programmers to think about error handling in advance. We need to consider problems we may face and think how to "catch" them so that they can be fixed.

In this chapter, however, we'll focus on methods that deal with errors over which we have no control. Syntax errors and spelling errors are easily fixed nowadays because the development environment warns you about the problem and even autocorrects it or suggests the solution. What we need to prepare for is real error handling, which refers to fixing the program's environment after set guidelines, not fixing the code necessarily.

Exceptions

One of the main problems you'll encounter in any programming language is the exception. This is an error that has nothing to do with your programming. It's a problem that happens in the real world due to factors outside of your control and the user needs to deal with them so that the program can function correctly. For instance, let's say that your program needs to open a file. It's a basic operation that looks something like this:

myVariable = open (myFile)

print (myVariable.name)

Just add your own variable name and the file name you're interested in. Remember that if the file in question is in the same folder or directory as the code, we don't have to specify the file's path. Now, let's say we have only one such file, called "employees.csv" and it contains data on a company's staff. We don't care about the information itself. The first line of code opens the file and the second prints the name of the file. Now, what if we run our program by right clicking on the Python file and selecting to run it inside the Console in order to show that specific file and open it? Think about it. We're assuming that we have a file with that particular name inside our folder. This is where we need to think about handling exceptions.

Now, let's say that the file we planned to access is no longer in the same folder because someone moved it, deleted it, or renamed it. After all, haven't you ever moved or changed a file by accident? If anything like this happened, then the program will throw an exception. This is a fancy, technical way of saying that it shows us an error message. The exception in our example would look something like this:

Traceback (most recent call last):

```
File "c:/ Users/ Admin/ Desktop/ exceptions/ myprogram.py", line 2,

in <module>

thefile = open('employees.csv')

FileNotFoundError: [Errno 2]

No such file or directory: 'employees.csv'
```

Let's break the exception apart and discuss each element. The traceback refers to a scenario in which we would have more than one exception, where they would all be displayed in the order they occurred. However, here we only have one. The "File" is what lets us know the location of the exception, namely the second line of our program file. The "thefile" section clearly tells us which is the culprit, namely the bit of code that causes the error. Lastly, we have the exception which is a simple "file not found error".

Most exceptions come with a number attached because they're different depending on the user's operating system. However, we don't need that to handle the errors. Instead, the "FileNotFoundError" part tells us everything we need to know. Even the "Errno 2" is irrelevant in most cases. Finally, the last part describes what happened. The program couldn't locate the specified file, and therefore couldn't open it because it doesn't exist in that folder.

An easy way to fix this issue would be changing the program by correcting the name of the file or its path so that the app can find it. The most common problem when dealing with csv files is the fact that the extension is wrongly declared. When you type fast it's very easy to overlook the name and type cvs instead. You might consider just renaming the file, or you can instruct the program to look for the misspelled version. It's up to you. You can even be more creative and use a loop to look for the illusive file (just don't do that in the real world). Mistakes happen, but Python alerts us, and if we can read the raised exception, then we immediately get the clue on how to solve the problem.

On a final note, you might hear the terms "raising an exception" or "throwing an exception". They mean exactly the same thing. The program encounters an error and tells you what happened. There's no difference between the two, it just depends on how each programmer learned the theory.

Dealing With Errors

In order to better handle program errors and exceptions, it's best to change what Python displays by default. Keep in mind that at the end of the day it's the user's experience that matters, not the programmer's vision. Achieving perfection is close to impossible, but you can give your program the ability to make your user understand what's going on when something unexpected happens. That is why in programming we have the so-called "try/except" blocks. The syntax is simple:

try:

Add what your program is supposed to do, except for the following

Exception:

Now, instruct the app on what to do if something mentioned above isn't possible for whatever reason.

Let's grab our earlier example and instruct the application to deal with a file that can't be found:

try:

myFile = open ('employees.csv')

print(myFile.name)

except Exception:

print ("Oops, I can't find any file named employees.csv in here")

What we do is attempt to open the file, as stated in the "try" section. If the file is opened, then the command within the try statement will be executed and the file will be opened and displayed. However, if the program raises an exception, then it won't just close with a default error. It will display a message that clearly explains what happens so that any user without programming knowledge can understand.

Specific Exceptions

In the previous section we dealt with the typical "file not found" error, however, we can do better than that. For instance, instead of just displaying the error message, we could use our problem solving skills to rename the file correctly and successfully execute the application again, this time without an error. Let's go back to our code and add a new line of code, just below the print statement:

try:

myFile = open ('employees.csv')

print (myFile.name)

print (myFile.itguys())

except Exception:

print("Oops, I can't find any file named employees.csv in here")

If we execute the code, we'll still see this:

employees.csv

Oops, I can't find any file named employees.csv in here.

The file was found since its name has been printed, but then we still get our error message. What's going on? The issue here is inside the exception block, which translates to "once an exception is thrown inside the try block, run this code here". This is bad because the error is due to the new line we introduced. Python doesn't have any element called "itguys". So, we need to change the exception block. We need to refine it to precisely detect the problem it needs to catch. But how can we figure out such a thing ahead of time? In fact, it's quite simple.

Go back to the original "FileNotFoundError"; that's where the clue is. The first part of it tells us the name of the exception and we can use it like so:

try:

myFile = open ('employees.csv')

print(myFile.name)

print(myFile.itguys())

except FileNotFoundError:

print ("Oops, I can't find any file named employees.csv in here")

Keep in mind that this modification won't do anything for our obviously terrible method that we introduced. But that doesn't matter in this case, because the method is in fact a programming error and not an exception. Therefore, we just need to change it with an adequate method that exists and does something. The previous error is no longer there and that's what matters. The program works and we only see the easy to fix "object has no attribute 'itguys'" error message instead. Don't try to fix this with the exception handling method.

Remember that exceptions are triggered only when something outside of the application is causing a problem because the app depends on it. Programming errors are fixed by directly changing the code. In this case, you can simply remove the method since it's not doing anything anyway.

Is Your Program Crashing?

Other errors can be fixed using except statements inside the try block. You just need to know that when an exception is raised, it will first check the statement at the top. If you encounter an exception that you didn't handle, you'll see a default message. However, we can solve that problem too and avoid such error messages altogether.

In order to eliminate every single default error message, we need to have a final exception that catches everything else that went through our previous exceptions. In the following example you'll notice that there are two exception handlers. One is specifically written for the "file not found" type of error, while the other is supposed to handle every other error.

try:

myFile = open ('employees.csv')

Let's print a few empty lines right before the first actual line.

print ('\n\n', myFile.readline())

Next, we'll close the file.

myFile.closed()

except FileNotFoundError:

print ("Oops, I can't find any file named employees.csv in here")

except Exception:

print ("Oops, I don't know what happened, but something else went bonkers!")

Here's the output of this code:

Username, FirstName, LastName, Role, DateCreated,

Oops, I don't know what happened, but something else went bonkers!

In the first line of the output we have whatever is found in the first line inside the file we just opened. The second result is the error message from the exception. The problem here is that we can't do anything because we don't have enough information. The error message isn't descriptive at all. Instead of being confused by an unknown error, we need to insert the message into a variable and then display its data. In programming it's common practice to name this variable "err" or "e", but as with all variables you can name it however you see fit.

Now, let's modify the code we just wrote. We need to place any captured exception and therefore its error message inside a variable and then print it:

```
try:

myFile = open ('employees.csv')

# Let's print a few empty lines right before the first actual line.

print ('\n\n', myFile.readline())

myFile.itguys()



except FileNotFoundError:

print ("Oops, I can't find any file named employees.csv in here")

except Exception as e:

print(e)
```

If we execute the code, we should see something like this:

Username, FirstName, LastName, Role, DateCreated,

'_io.TextIOWrapper' object has no attribute 'itguys'

The first line is what we expected, namely the contents of the file we opened. No error is raised, the file is found, so it's all good. However, the second line may seem a bit strange. You may not understand what it's telling you, but it's already miles ahead of a generic "something happened" kind of message. What we have now is enough to describe the problem. We now definitely know there's something wrong with the "itguys" attribute.

What's most important is that the error was handled and the program didn't crash. It's still running just fine, despite the problem. Furthermore, we now have evidence about an error that is easily fixable. Even if this might not help the end user, it provides information to the team behind the program or to tech support so that the error can be patched. When developing software in the real world, we have to think further than just getting our idea to work.

Improving the "Try" Syntax

If you take a moment to examine some code written by the pros (you should totally do that), their try blocks are very clean without too much code cluttering them. The reason is that they use catch blocks to handle errors that may occur. These blocks are meant to handle an exception if it exists, but if it doesn't then the program will just ignore them and continue executing the rest of the code. Here's how the syntax looks for this improved error handling method:

try: Insert whatever you think might cause an error.

catch (typical exception that occurs often): Explain the exception.

catch exception as err:

Display a standard error message.

else:

Continue with this code if no error is detected.

In other words, if our file isn't found, the process stops and displays the error. Otherwise, the code keeps running. If we add a limit to the try block, specifically to the one that is more likely to throw the exception, the code will stop being executed. However, if there's no exception being thrown, then it will continue as the else block states. Here's a full example:

try:

Open the file.

myFileile = open ('employees.csv')

Look for a frequently occurring error and stop the application from running.

```python
except FileNotFoundError:

print ("Oops, I can't find any file named employees.csv in here")

# Catch the exception and stop the program.

except Exception as e:

print(e)

# If no error is found then continue running the application as normal.

else:

# Since no exception was raised, the program found the file and everything works
fine.

# Print a blank line.

print('\n')

# Print the lines from the file we opened.

for some_lines in myFile:

print(some_lines)

myFile.close()

print ("Good job!")
```

Handle Exceptions Like a Pro

If you analyzed someone else's code to get a better idea on how exception handling is done in real world applications, you may have noticed that there's one more syntax element we can add:

try:

Try to perform these operations

except:

If this happens, stop running the program at this point.

except Exception as e:

If anything else bad happens, then stop here instead.

else:

If there are no errors to worry about, continue with the operating from here and ignore the previous blocks.

finally:

Execute these lines no matter whether there were any errors above or not.

This new component is the "finally" block. If we introduce this in our exception handling code, anything we insert inside it will be processed no matter what. Keep in mind that this is optional and usually it's used in complex programs that involve certain bits of code to rely on the existence of some external elements that may or may not exist. If those elements are found, the code is executed, but if not then some other operations are executed instead. Let's go through such an example to help you visualize what we're talking about:

print('Show this line first.')

try:

open ('employees.csv')

except FileNotFoundError:

print ('Oops, I can't find any file named employees.csv in here')

except Exception as err:

print('err')

else:

print ('If no exception is found, show this line.')

finally:

print('Now we're in the finally block.')

When you execute the program, the file will be found and the output will look like this:

Show this line first.

If no exception is found, show this line.

Now we're in the finally block.

No exception was raised because the file was found. As you can see, the finally block was printed as well. Now execute the code, but this time remove the file the program is looking for. You'll see that the app will tell you the file can't be found, but we won't experience a crash. Instead, it will keep running the code that follows.

Summary

Learning to use these try, else, finally, exception raising blocks will help you have better control over your program. You should focus on using exception handling methods in areas of your application where you think the user will cause the error for any reason that is outside the functionality of your program. That way, the program won't crash, but will continue running the rest of operations as normal.

Chapter 5:

How to Work with External Files

Everything that you store on your computer is in the form of a file. Text documents, images, videos, applications, games, you name it. These files are usually stored in folders, or directories, depending on your computer's operating system. To find them and access then you can use applications like the Windows File Explorer, or Mac's Finder. However, when working with code and developing software, you need to know different ways of accessing these files. So, in this chapter, you are going to learn all about Python's tools that allow us to create, read, and write a variety of files and how to work with them using pure code.

Binary and Text

Files can be classified into two distinct categories:

1.   Binary Files: These files are used to store computer data in the form of bytes. This is the computer's native language, so whatever you see in these files is unreadable to your eyes. Well, actually, you can learn binary and figure out what every combination of 0 and 1 means, but realistically you don't want to go through that. On a side note, if you open this kind of file using a text editor, you'll see a bunch of unreadable gibberish. For instance, you can open an image file inside a text editor and you'll see text, just not in characters you're familiar with. The text won't mean anything to you, but you can read it. Just don't save and overwrite that file in text or you can cause some issues.

Binary files include the following examples: Executable files (.exe, .bin), images (jpg, gif), pdf documents, compressed zip files, mp3 audio files, videos, and fonts.

2.   Text Files: These files are readable because they contain characters. So when you run them inside an editor, you'll see the text characters you're used to. However, this doesn't mean you'll understand what you're reading because they might not be set in a particular language.

       Text files include the following examples: Simple text files like .txt and .csv, source code files like your Python files, and data (json or xml).

The file types we mention are the most common ones you're certainly familiar with. There are other files that are split into these two categories.

Before we get started with practical examples, take note that in this chapter we're going to use Visual Studio Code as our coding editor instead of the usual Jupyter notebook, Vim or the online Python console. You may have heard of of Visual Studio being used normally with other languages like C#, but it also offers Python support. You don't have to use this editor, though. Any will do just fine. The reason why we're going to play around with it in this chapter is because it has a handy Explorer bar to show us the folder/directory we're in.

Open and Close Files from Python

The first thing you need to learn is how to open and close files using Python code. You already did this in the previous chapter where we attempted to open a csv file, but there's more to it than just that. With that being said, the more complete syntax looks like this:

open (myfile.ext [,mode])

Replace the placeholder for the file accordingly; just remember that this works if the file is in the same folder as your Python source code file. If it's not, then you'll also have to mention the path of the file you're trying to access. For instance, if you're using a Windows operating system, you'll have to use forward slashes like this:

C:/Users/Admin/Desktop/cat.png.

Notice that in code we aren't using backslashes like you'd see in the path inside the File Explorer.

The "mode" part of the syntax isn't obligatory. Its purpose is to define the access level of your application. Inside the brackets you can place an instruction that tells Python what it can do with the file. Here's a summary:

1. Read [r]: This gives the program permission to open and read the file. This means that no modifications can be made. By default, this is the permission level Python has so there's no need to mention it.

2. Read and Write [r+]: The program will be able to read and write to the file.

3. Write [w]: Changes can be made to the file and if it can't be found, a new one will be created.

4. Append [a]: Python will open the file and introduce new content. This is different from the writing privileges because the program won't be allowed to change existing information, just add to it.

5. Create [x]: The app will create a new file. Take note that if the file with the same specified name exists, Python will raise a FileExistsError exception.

In addition to the modes, we can also instruct our program to open, create, or modify a specific file type. This is done the same way by adding the letter "t" for text files or "b" for binary files.

Now, the "open" method can actually be used in another way as well. The first thing we can do is assigned a variable to the file as a reference so that we can refer to it whenever we want:

myVariable = open (myfile.ext [,mode])

While you can use any variable you want as usual, most Python programmers use the letter "f" because it makes it clear that we're dealing with a file. This isn't an official rule, but more of an unofficial standard followed by most. The problem, however, is that this example isn't the best. The problem is that when Python opens the file, it stays that way until we add the "close" method to close it. And if we don't close the file, we can encounter later issues by having a large number of open files at the same time and cause the program to crash or throw exceptions. So, make sure to use the close method if you choose this syntax.

Once we open the file, we need to gain access to the data. We'll be discussing this in detail, but right now we're interested in just copying the information inside the file. The easiest way to do that is placing the content of the file inside a variable and then displaying it with the print function. Here's how all of this works in code:

```
f = open ('mytextfile.txt')

filecontent = f.read()

print(filecontent)
```

Remember, the file remains open until we close it, so make sure to use the close method like this:

```
f.close ()
```

The bottom line is that if a file is unnecessary, it shouldn't be open. There's no need to waste resources or risk the program encountering a problem you never anticipated.

Another way of opening the file is through something called "contextual coding" or the context manager. To use this method, we need the keyword "with" and only later in the code we create a variable. The same line needs to be ended with a colon in order to tell Python where the with block should start. The advantage of using this method is that we don't have to use the close method anymore. Here's an example of contextual syntax:

```
with open ('mytextfile.txt') as f:

filecontent = f.read()

print(filecontent)
```

You can use either method since both of them are fine. However, most programmers choose the contextual syntax, and this book will do so as well because of the fewer things that can go wrong. So, it would probably be best if you'd just go with the unofficial standard as well and get a solid footing from the get go.

Now, our example works just fine because it's a text file. Let's see what happens in the following example:

with open ('funny_cat.jpg') as f:

filecontent = f.read()

print (filecontent)

This will result in an error that looks like this:

UnicodeDecodeError: 'charmap' codec can't decode byte 0x90 in position 40: character maps to <undefined>

The message doesn't mean much, but the problem is clear. We used the 'f' mode, trying to open the file as a text file when we're dealing with a jpg file, an image. As mentioned earlier, images are binary files, so we need to open the file in 'b' mode:

with open ('funny_cat.jpg', 'b') as f:

filecontent = f.read()

print(filecontent)

Now, if you run this program, we'll no longer get an error, but we'll still not see an image. Instead we're going to see a lot of gibberish like this:

\xb5\xba\xb5\x00\xfa\xf9,\x8c\xe2\x89(p\x07\xdd{\xd9,\x0e\xc2\x81<N\
xe1\xb05\xa0\xc4`a\xc1\xb59\xbe}\xc6@k\xe4\xb1\x8d\xa1\xe3\xd8\xfc,x
\x87\xc3\xdb\xd1ch\xd9\xe8\x84OaZ\xf7\xb2\x11'\xec\xce\xe9\xfbX\xb2
\xca4\x00\xaaw\xcf\xd1Q

Instead, if you open the same file inside Visual Studio, or a dedicated graphics display editor, you're going to see a regular picture. The reason why we don't get a display of the image using the print function is because it prints the bytes that are the building blocks of the file. This isn't a graphic display application, so all we get is gibberish even though it's not an error or something along those lines. Let's see a different example

with open ('encodednames.txt') as f:

filecontent = f.read()

print (filecontent)

Again, we open a text file, but we encounter an error like we did when opening the image file:

UnicodeDecodeError: 'charmap' codec can't decode byte 0x81 in position 45: character maps to <undefined>

But both files are text! We can see that because of the .txt file extension. That's true, but some text files don't display the typical characters you're used to (ASCII). Some of them used UTF-8 characters on top of them. In order to open this file, we need to instruct our application to look out for these characters using UTF encoding. So, we need to edit the first line to make it look like this:

with open ('encodednames.txt', 'r', encoding = 'utf-8') as f:

Now when Python opens the file, we'll be able to read it because the odd characters are essentially "translated" to what we can understand.

So, what's UTF-8 and what's the point, you might ask? UTF stands for Unicode Transformation format, which is in 8-bit, and its purpose is to represent letters and numbers on machines. ASCII, the typical letters, numbers, and punctuation marks you're used to, are no longer enough nowadays, especially when we consider other languages. UTF-8 is an agreed upon international standard in handling multiple languages and is used as the main character set on all things that are on the Internet. That is why you'll frequently encounter it.

So to summarize this section, whenever you open files you need to keep the following things in mind:

1. Plain text files written in ASCII can be opened with "r" as the specified mode.

2. Binary files are opened with the letter 'b' in the mode.

3. If you're looking at a text file but you can't understand it, you are probably dealing with a UTF-8 encoded file, so specify that in the "open" declaration.

Reading the Data

At the beginning of this chapter we used the 'read' method to read the data inside our files. That's isn't the only approach. In fact, we can use 3 options.

1. read ([size]): With this method we can read the whole file if we don't declare a specific size. If we do, then the program will read a set number of characters if it's a text file, or a set number of bytes if it's a binary file.

2. readline: This method allows our program to read a single line of data. The end of that line is considered at the beginning of a newline character.

3. readlines: Don't misspell or confuse this method with the previous one. This one will read all the lines.

Take note that since nobody types in binary, if there are any newline characters inside binary files, they are just random. That is why method number two and three should only be used on text files. Furthermore, the 'read' and 'readline' methods enable the program to read the whole file. The main difference between the two is that the first method reads all the information as a whole, while the second one goes through each line at a time and stores them as list items. Here's an example:

with open ('famous_proverbs.txt') as f:

content = f.read()

print (content)

The variable we created will store everything and if we print it, we'll see the information contained within. You'll notice that the content is divided in several lines just like the text file, because every line ends with a newline character and therefore there's a new line when the data is displayed. Now, let's see an example with the 'readline' method instead:

```
with open('famous_proverbs.txt') as f:

content = f.readlines()

print(content)
```

You'll see that the result has square brackets surrounding it. That means we're dealing with a list. Inside the list, each object is separated by commas and encapsulated in quotation marks. Where one object ends, we have a newline character to refer to the end of the line.

As for the readline method, as mentioned it only reads a single line at a time. The line is extended from the start of the file to the end of a newline character. In order to read the line that follows, we would need to run another readline method. Here's how it works in code:

```
with open('famous_proverbs.txt') as f:

content = f.readline()

print(content)
```

The result will be the first line of your file and that's it. Due to the nature of the "readline" and "readlines" methods, we should be using loops in order to access and manipulate the data, otherwise we would end up with a mess.

Looping Through Files

We can use the 'readlines' and 'readline' methods to loop through files. Don't forget that 'readlines' already reads the file as an entire construct, but this poses a problem. If your program has to deal with a massive file, the computer might run out of memory before the whole file can be read. That is why you should use this option if you're sure the file isn't bigger than several hundred lines of content so you can access the data fast. However, the information will be stored inside a list, so we still need to loop through the list instead of the original file. Take note that we can also loop through binary files. The difference is that they don't have lines of text, so they're read in blocks instead of lines.

Now, let's see how we can loop through the list once we read all the data with readlines:

with open ('famous_proverbs.txt') as f:

Reading the lines and then looping through them.

for one_line in f.readlines():

print (one_line)

When you execute this code, you'll notice that we have double spaces due to the fact that all list objects end with a newline character and the print statement also adds a newline character every time it loops. In order to have single spaces we should change the print statement like this:

print (one_line, end=")

Now, let's say you're dealing with a file containing names, so you want to print the names indented with a space and an empty line to seperate it from the next. The easiest way to achieve that is with the enumerate function. When we use enumerate with a list, the function will count how many times we loop through the list. To clarify, we won't use the same for loop we used above. Instead, we'll write the loop as "for one_line in enumerate (f.readlines()):" and every single pass will record the line count. As the program passes through a loop, you'll notice the counter. So, here's how the code itself will look:

with open('quotes.txt') as f:

Reading the lines and then looping through them.

The count will start from zero.

for one_line in enumerate (f.readlines()):

When the count reaches an even number, we won't print an additional newline.

if one_line[0] % 2 == 0:

print(one_line[1], end=")

In any other case we will have an additional newline and extra spaces.

else:

print (' ' + one_line[1])

As mentioned earlier, using "readlines" involves taking a chance if you don't fully know under which circumstances your program will run. If the app has to process an enormous file, it's going to require quite a bit of RAM. So, in fact, you have to think about two unknowns: the size of the file, and the amount of RAM the computer running the program has. If there isn't enough memory, the program will simply crash. So, what's probably best to do is looping line after line. This method will barely use any memory during processing. To do this we need to open the file, read a single line, and then store it inside a variable. The purpose of the loop is to keep cycling through the file as long as we don't have an empty variable. In other words, we need a while loop. Since we're dealing with a text file, every single line of content is going to have some text. This means that our variable will only be empty once there are no more lines to handle.

At this point you should be writing your own code because you know enough about file access and looping. Remember, this is the only real way to learn programming. You know the plan, so try and execute it on your own. If you're struggling, you can come back and check the following code:

```
with open ('famous_proverbs.txt') as f:

one_line = f.readline()

while one_line:

print (one_line, end='')

one_line = f.readline()
```

The only "danger" involving this method is forgetting to run the readline function within the loop in order to progress. If you make such a mistake, you'll end up with an infinite loop that will keep printing the first line. If this happens, don't worry, you don't have to crash the program or something so drastic in order to stop the loop. Just hit the Ctrl + C keys and the program will exit the loop.

To Append or Overwrite?

Whenever you deal with files, you need to be aware of what appending and writing mean. You don't want to accidentally overwrite some important data and lose it forever. For instance, if you have a file with some content and you modify it while in write mode, you won't just introduce more information to the file, you'll in fact overwrite it. And no, there's no undo button for this action. So, if you make a mistake like this, you can lose data. Instead, you need to open the file in the append mode and then use the write method to add new information without deleting what's already there.

To illustrate this method, imagine having a file with a list of names and we need to introduce a new one. The new name, as well as the existing ones, will also contain characters that aren't found in English, but in other languages like German. This means that we'll also need that UTF-8 encoding we talked about earlier. In addition, we want to format the file somewhat and have a newline at the end of any new name we introduce to the list. Here's how this works in practice:

This is where we add a new name with a newline at the end.

added_name = 'Jacob Hülsen Schöpfer\n'

Open your file using the append mode (a) and don't forget encoding.

with open ('myfile.txt', 'a', encoding='utf-8') as f:

f.write(added_name)

To see if this works properly, you should continue with code that doesn't contain any indentation. This way the file will be closed automatically by the program. Then we can open in read mode and see what it contains, using the following lines:

The file we opened is now closed.

print ('nSuccess')

Now we can read the file again to verify the content. Don't forget encoding.

with open ("myfile.txt", encoding='utf-8') as f:

print (f.read())

Dealing with CSV Files

As mentioned earlier in this book, CSV files are typically used because they allow us to store information in the form of tabular data. In other words, we're dealing with spreadsheets divided in rows and columns. Examples of such files can be found from tabular applications such as Microsoft Excel and Google Sheets. Without such programs, we wouldn't have any tabular format because regular text files would just display each row as a line. However, these files are usable in our case because the text editor will separate each value and we still have the headers in the very first line of the file. Furthermore, names are usually written in between quotation marks and the commas used to separate the first name from the last name doesn't mark the beginning of a new column because of the quotation marks, like this:

"John, Smith", 1990

The second column is marked by the comma outside of the quotes. Take note that depending on the text editor, you may see double or single quotation marks encapsulating the string, but either of them work. This can cause a problem when single quotes are used and we have names that involve an apostrophe:

'Jack, O'Neill'

Python sees an 'O' but then it doesn't know what to do with the rest of the string. That is why double quotation marks should be used instead.

Working with CSV files can sometimes be even more tricky because there are other issues you can encounter. For instance, if you have to deal with names written with characters that aren't part of the ASCII set. In some cases, you might have a line with nothing but three dots. If your table involves financial records, you'll probably have dollar signs and commas in between digits and that won't work with Python's floats. That is why we need to discuss this topic because tabular data, even though it's text, is somewhat different from the previous text files we explored.

You can work with CSV files in two ways. You either take the manual route and use everything you learned so far, or you can import Python's csv module to give you all the tools you need. Just type "import csv" at the top of your application and you'll extend Python's functionality.

Opening the File

To open a CSV file, you can use the same methods discussed above. After all, it's a text file so it's subjected to the same rules. There's just a higher chance of such files containing non-ASCII characters, so make sure you add the utf-8 encoding. In addition, since this is tabular data, you probably won't want to use newline characters after every single row, in which case you could add "newline=""" inside the open statement instead. Here's all this in action:

Opening a CSV file using UTF-8 encoding

with open ('mydata.csv', encoding='utf-8', newline='') as f:

Next, we might be interested in looping through the file. For this operation we can use an existing reader function that reads each row during the execution.

reader = csv.reader(f)

Since tabular data is divided into rows, we should also count them as the program reads the data. Remember the enumerate function we used earlier? That's going to come in handy to achieve just that:

Introducing the row counter and reader.

reader = enumerate (csv.reader(f))

The next step is to modify to loop so it reads a single row at a time. Take note that since we have an enumerator, we'll have two variables inside our loop. One is needed to track the counter from zero, and the second will hold a whole table row:

In the modified loop, n is the counter and myRow represents the row.

for n, myRow in reader:

Now we can continue with a print statement to display the value of our n and myRow variables everytime we cycle through the loop. Here's the full example:

import csv

with open ('mydata.csv', encoding='utf-8', newline='') as f:

Introducing the row counter and reader.

reader = enumerate(csv.reader(f))

In the modified loop, n is the counter and myRow represents the row.

for n, myRow in reader:

print(n, myRow)

print('Success')

The result will look something like this:

0 ['\ufeffFull Name', 'Year of Birth', 'Date Created', 'Is Valid', 'Balance']

1 ['Smith, John', '1980', '3/12/2012', 'TRUE', '$450.00']

2 ['Doe, James', '1978', '22/11/2010', 'FALSE', '-$134.00']

3 ['', '', '', '', '']

...

The data will depend on your own file's contents. But what we will always have is row 0 which is the header containing the names of the columns. You'll notice, however, that at the start of the header we have "\ufeff". This is something known as a Byte Order Mark and it's typical to Microsoft Excel. There's no need to be concerned with it because the content of the header doesn't matter. The actual information is inside the rows that come after.

As you can see in our example, we have five objects separated by commas. Due to this aspect, Python allows us to access the information in each column by declaring its position. So for instance, myRow[1] will refer to the year of birth. Don't forget that in programming, position 0 is always the first. Furthermore, all the information in the tabular file consists of strings even when you might not see them that way. No matter what, a CSV file will contain string data simply because this kind of file is a text file, and text files are made out of strings, not Booleans and integers. However, Python allows us to convert this string data into any other data type we may need. We're going to focus on this topic in the coming sections.

How to Convert Strings

Since CSV files already contain string data items, we don't actually have to convert them into strings. However, we still need to handle certain empty strings or break other larger strings into smaller ones.

The main thing we're interested in is data. This excludes the first row because it doesn't contain any. It's just a description of the columns. Therefore, we're going to start with an if conditional inside a loop and tell the program not to run anything when we're in the first row (row 0).

Ignore the row that contains nothing other than column headings.

if n > 0:

full_name = myRow[0].split(',')

last_name = full_name[0].strip()

first_name = full_name[1].strip()

The code is really basic. All it tells the program is that as long as it doesn't search inside the first row, a variable called "full_name" should be created to store the data found inside the first column. This data is also divided into two values separated by a comma. Once Python runs this code, the last name found inside the "full_name[0]" column is placed into a new variable called "full_name". The same happens with the first name which is also placed in the corresponding variable. This is how you can divide a string into two variables to gain more control over your CSV data. However, if you execute the program now, you'll get an error. Why? Go back to the CSV content and you'll notice that inside row number three we don't have a full name. We have an empty string which can't be divided. We need to fix this.

To solve this issue, we need to instruct Python to divide the name if possible when encountering the comma. If it doesn't work, we'll need to store an empty string inside all three name variables. In the next example we'll make these modifications and we'll no longer print the n variable and the entire row, but instead just the first and last names.

```
import csv

with open ('mydata.csv', encoding='utf-8', newline='') as f:

reader = enumerate (csv.reader(f))

for i, myRow in reader:

if i > 0:

try:

full_name = myRow[0].split(',')

last_name = full_name[0].strip()

first_name=full_name[1].strip()

except IndexError:

full_name = last_name = first_name = ""

print(first_name, last_name)

print('Success!')
```

Now it all works as intended with no errors.

From Strings to Integers

In the second column of our CSV file we have a number representing the birth year. As mentioned, this is a string, but it contains the kind of data that we could convert into an integer instead. Brush up your knowledge of the int function, because we're going to use it. However, we'll still have the same issues as before regarding row number 3 which is empty. Our application won't convert it automatically to 0, so we need to do something about it. Here's how we'll proceed:

birth_year= int(row[1] or 0)

That's it! One line of code is all we needed. What this translates to is an instruction that tells Python to create a new variable and place it inside the second column if possible. If there's no value that can be converted to an integer, then it will be stored in a 0.

Now, let's see how we're going to handle our third column, which is a date, though at the moment it's a string in the current format.

From Strings to Date

The third column contains dates, except for the third row which is again without any data. In order to convert this string information into a date datatype, we'll have to use the datetime module once again. Once we do that, the actual conversion is simple:

import datetime as dt

date_created = dt.datetime.strptime(row[2],"%m/%d/%Y").date()

Well, this may be one line of code, but its simplicity actually involves quite a bit of information. As usual, we started by importing the module we need and declaring a variable. The first thing that pops out is "strptime" which stands for "string parse for datetime". Then we specify that we're interested in the third column and instruct the program with the "%m/%d/%Y" syntax that we have a month, day, and year format separated by slashes. The final bit at the end of the line "date" instructs Python that we're only interested in date information, without the time.

Once again, row number 3 will pose a problem because it contains no data so we're going to get an error. This time we are going to use a try block and if we can't get the date, we'll use a "none" value which Python recognizes as an empty object. Remember that datetime is in fact a class. This means that all dates and times are actually objects belonging to that class. So, here's what we can do about this conversion:

```
import csv

import datetime

with open ('mydata.csv', encoding='utf-8', newline='') as f:

reader = enumerate(csv.reader(f))

for i, row in reader:

if i > 0:

try:

full_name = row[0].split(',')

last_name = full_name[0].strip()

first_name = full_name[1].strip()

except IndexError:

full_name = last_name = first_name = ""

birth_year = int(row[1] or 0)

try:
```

```
date_created = datetime.datetime.strptime(row[2], "%m/%d/%Y").date()
```

```
except ValueError:
```

```
date_created = None
```

```
print(first_name, last_name, birth_year, date_created)
```

```
print('Success')
```

No more error and the output looks fine. Next up, we have to deal with the Boolean values inside the fourth column.

From Strings to Boolean

Our CSV file contains a TRUE or FALSE result inside the fourth column. Take note that in this example we have these values written in uppercase letters just because Microsoft Excel likes them that way and when saving to a CSV file the format is kept. Your tabular data may differ depending on the program you used. Python likes those values only with the first letter written in uppercase. With that in mind, we are going to convert the string values to Boolean with the help of the bool function. Luckily, this is going to be extremely simple because row number 3 won't cause us any issues this time. Python will consider the empty cell as False by default. So, the code will simply look like this:

```
is_active = bool(row[3])
```

That's it!

From Strings to Floats

Finally, we have the balance data inside the fifth column, which is represented by an amount expressed in US dollars. Normally, you want this kind of information to be converted to a float, but there are a couple of issues we need to figure out. First is the dollar sign, which isn't accepted into a float. The second one is the comma, which is also not accepted in floats. So, we need to remove both of them from the data before performing the conversion. In addition, trailing spaces are also unacceptable, but they are automatically removed with the strip method.

In the following line of code, we are going to create and designate a variable for the balance string data, but without the comma and dollar sign:

```
balance_string = (row[4].replace('$','').replace(',','')).strip()
```

In the next line we will tell Python that the string variable we created will contain the data inside the fifth column. Afterwards we're going to use the float method to convert the string variable into a float variable. Here's the final piece of the puzzle:

```
final_balance = float (balance_string or 0)

print(first_name, last_name, birth_year, date_created, is_valid, balance)
```

Now, you can connect all the pieces together and have an application that fully converts each string element inside our tabular data to appropriate data types we can later manipulate.

JSON Data

9,05,
5,94,66755.39,0,0,0,
59,12,42826.99,0,0,0,0,30
35,64,50656.8,0,0,0,0,30
115,94,67905.07,0,0,0,0,30
115,94,66938.9,0,0,0,0,
0192,49,86421.04,0,0,0,
73798 5,

JavaScript Object Notation is a frequently used marshalling format for object oriented programming. If you aren't familiar with the term 'marshalling', it refers to a specific format that is used to transfer information between computers. However, certain databases are capable of storing directly in JSON format.

You may have heard of JavaScript, the programming language, and maybe you're wondering why we're talking about it when we're using Python. No worries, you don't have to start learning a new language just yet. JSON simply started with JavaScript so they are related, even though we're talking about the format that is used in different programming languages and various computer systems.

In this section we are going to focus on JSON data and on how to transfer it in and out. As we go through this topic, discussing the major concepts and functionality, you'll notice that this type of data is in fact very similar to the dictionaries you use in Python. So, if you already practiced with dictionaries enough, you won't have to learn too much new theory. In addition, working with JSON data in Python is easy because Python already provides us with the JSON module which contains a number of useful functions and methods.

JSON data is easier to understand if you compare it to the data inside a standard spreadsheet, like the ones from Excel. The data written in JSON format is just data that's been converted to key/value pairs, meaning it's dictionary data. Another option is to obtain keyed JSON files where every block of information has one unique key to work as its identifier. This key is either represented by some text or a number. Take note that when you download someone's JSON files they are usually keyed. For instance, if a website relies on Google Firebase Realtime Database to keep track of certain information about the activity, the database will store data using generated keys that look like a random sequence of numbers and letters. If you check one of these files, you'll also notice that it doesn't follow the same date format as an Excel file. Instead, it'll use serial dates.

The Concept of Serialization

One of the most important concepts related to JSON is something known as serialization. This is a process of converting an object such as a dictionary to a sequence of characters that can be transferred and stored inside the computer's memory or a database. The purpose of this feature is to save the data inside the object in such a way that we can obtain it and access it from any other system. When doing so, the data is converted back to an object. This process is referred to as deserialization. If this feels a bit too confusing, we can summarize it like this:

1. Serialization: Turn any object into a string of characters.

2. Deserialization. Turn the string back into an object.

As mentioned earlier, when working with JSON files we need to use the json modules provided in Python's library. Keep in mind this is a normal module already included, so we just need to import it as with all the other modules at the start of our code. The module will provide us with four main json methods:

1. dump: This will write Python information into a JSON file. This is a serializing method.

2. dumps: This method writes Python objects to JSON character strings. It is also a serializing method.

3. load: The purpose of this method is to load JSON information from files or objects. This is a deserializing method.

4. loads: This method will load JSON information from inside a character string. This is also a deserializing method.

A final note before switching to practice is that JSON data types are comparable to Python data types, however, they're not quite alike. Here's a list with each Python dictionary and its equivalent in JSON:

1.   dict = object

2.   list and tuple = array

3.   str = string

4.   integer and float = number

5.   True = true

6.   False = false

7.   None = null

Now that we have some of the basic theory sorted, let's see how we can load data from a JSON file.

Load the Data

To start off, we need to import the json module. Afterwards we use the open method just like before. In addition, we should also include the UTF-8 encoding since in many such files we'll also have non-ASCII characters. All we need to do next is create a variable where we'll store the data and then we can use the "load" method to load all the data inside it. Here's an example:

import json

This is tabular data from an excel file without any keys.

filename = 'employees_excel_info.json'

Opening the file like in the previous examples.

with open (filename, 'r', encoding='utf-8', newline='') as f:

Use the json load method to load the file to an object.

employees = json.load(f)

By executing this code, we won't see anything printed to the screen. However, we can examine the employees object using a couple of methods, such as using the print function.

print (employees)

Everything stored in the variable will be displayed. Take note of the square brackets you should see inside the output because that shows us "employees" is a list. We can double check this result to make sure it's accurate by typing the following line:

print (type (employees))

Python should print "<class 'list'>", thus confirming that the object is a list. And since it's a list, that means we can loop through it and learn what each item is:

for x in employees:

print(type(x))

Here's the output:

<class 'dict'> <class 'dict'> <class 'dict'> <class 'dict'> <class 'dict'> <class 'dict'> <class 'dict'>

Now we know that every single employee item in the list is a dictionary. This means that inside the loop we can use a key to identify every single value.

for x in employees:

print (x['Full Name'], x['Birth Year'], x['Date Created'], x['Is Valid'], x['Balance'])

Our little program will show all the information contained within the JSON file, which originally came from an Excel file. Now we can manipulate the data as needed.

Changing Data

Since our JSON data is in the form of a data dictionary, you can work with it using the same functions, methods and concepts you learned in Chapter 2. As long as we loop through the dictionary using a key and variables for the values, we can modify any key/value pair with the following syntax:

myvalue ['mykey'] = new_data

The key and value are variables found in the loop. For instance, let's say we're looping through a dictionary that was built using the Firebase database. This would include a field called "last visit" which appears in the form of a UTC Timestamp value. This timestamp can be turned into a string, which in turn is recognized by Python. In the following example you can see how the loop is set up, where the new variable is created to contain this Timestamp as a Python date, and then the date format will also be adjusted.

for mykey, myvalue in hits.items():

Changing the Firebase Timestamp date format to a Python date.

pythondate   =
datetime.datetime.utcfromtimestamp(myvalue['lastvisit']/1000).date()

Inside our dictionary, replace the Firebase date with the Python date as a string.

myvalue['lastvisit']= f" {pythondate:%m/%d/%Y})"

Once the loop finishes cycling, the values inside the 'lastvisit' column will be replaced with dates in the standard Python format we're used to instead of the stranger timestamp format used by the Firebase database. Now, in order to delete data from the dictionary while looping through it, we need to use the following syntax:

pop ('mykey', None)

Instead of 'mykey' you should add the column you want to delete. So, for instance, if we want to delete all the "mykey" data from the dictionary that was created by the Firebase database, we need to introduce this line:

myvalue.pop('mykey', None)

Take note that any modifications you make to a Python dictionary won't affect the file or character string we used to load the JSON data. In order to create a new JSON data file we need to use the "dump" or "dumps" methods.

As a final note, JSON is a popular data storage format. That is why we briefly discussed this topic. Python contains many tools for creating, modifying, and working with JSON data. In this section, however, we only covered the basics since this isn't a JSON guide. So if you want to learn more, feel free to explore other resources and expand your knowledge beyond Python.

Summary

In this chapter we explored two often used external data files, namely CSV files and JSON files. Python programming isn't an enclosed circle, and you can't limit yourself to just the language. In the real world, no matter what you're going to pursue, you will use a combination of tools. Python fortunately provides us with many such tools that make it much easier for us to integrate outside data type, files, and information in general. In this chapter you learned about these tools that enable you to work with binary and text files, tabular data, and JSON data. There's a lot more on these topics, but for now, you have enough to get started working with these file types.

Chapter 6:

Python Libraries and Modules

So far, we explored the core functionality of Python and various components that are common to all programming languages no matter how you choose to use them. However, you already noticed that in many cases the core functionality isn't enough and we need to extend it. This is done through Python libraries and modules. Every single module is a collection of methods, functions, and classes that serve a specific purpose in a certain area. They allow us to fulfill our vision without being forced to recreate something that already exists. In this chapter, we are going to learn more about the power of modules and libraries. You need to know more about them whether or not you choose to be a programmer, and especially if you want to use your knowledge of Python to get into data science or machine learning.

The Standard Library

The standard library is basically everything you worked with so far and more. It's the core of Python that contains all the data types such as integer, string, list, dictionary, and others. All instances of these data types are in fact instances of a certain class that is defined inside that library. As an interesting fact, that's why the word instance is a synonym for object in Python. While an integer is a whole number, in Python (as well as other languages) it's also a data type. However, inside the library there's a class which defines it. Therefore, every single integer you declare is an instance deriving from that base class. Let's see an example of this.

We have the "type" function we used earlier to check the data type of a piece of information, kind of like this:

n = 5

print (type (n))

The result is: <class 'int'>

This confirms that the n variable is an integer and therefore it's an instance of the integer class that's defined inside the core library. Here's another example:

n = 'hello'

print (type (n))

The result is: <class 'str'>

The function confirms that n is a string deriving from the str class. We can check all data types this way and learn whether their instances of their class are found in the standard library.

In the next two sections we are going to explore two useful core functions, namely "dir" and "help". You always have access to them no matter what application you're building, and you can even use them inside the basic command prompt, not just an editor. These functions are part of the main library and they will help us navigate the intricate web of classes, functions, methods, attributes, and much more that is found inside Python's core functionality. So, let's start discussing these two handy functions before progressing to modules and packages.

The "dir" Function

The purpose of the "dir" function is to give us a list containing every single attribute that's linked to a data type. For instance, we mentioned the class str above, which states that a certain piece of information belongs to the string data type. We know for sure it's a data type, therefore an instance of the string class, especially if it uses the dir function like so:

dir(str)

Here's the output:

['__add__', '__class__', '__dir__', '__doc__', '__format__','__init__','capitalize', 'casefold', 'center', 'count', 'encode', 'endswith', 'find', ...]

Take note that we didn't include all functions that pop up in the output because there are quite a few and we're not going to memorize them. Just keep in mind that the built-in elements found between double underlines (also known as dunders) aren't always accessed directly because they can sometimes refer to special methods. For instance, the very first method "__add__" is actually called inside our code whenever we use the plus sign, in other words the addition operator. The other components that aren't dunder items are your typical functions that end with parentheses. Let's go back to our previous string example:

n = "Hello"

print (type (n), x.isalpha(), x.upper())

The result is: <class 'str'> True HELLO

First we get our confirmation that we're dealing with a string variable. This means that we use all the attributes that are related with the string class. This is why the dir function is so handy, because it shows all related attributes. For instance, the output for the "isalpha" function is True because our string contains alphabetic characters. Then the "upper" function is used to turn the string's characters into uppercase characters.

At this point you might be asking yourself how the "dir" function can help you if all it does is show you a bunch of keywords that may or may not mean anything to you. For instance, you can't really make a guess on how to use "expandtabs" or "encode" without having more information. Well, the purpose of this function isn't to teach you what each method, function, and attribute does. It's supposed to inform you about which ones are connected to a specific data type. To get more information about them, we have the "help" function.

The "help" Function

Python provides us with the help function so that we can learn the purpose of anything contained in the library by using this syntax:

help (something)

Just replace the placeholder in the parentheses with whatever you're interested in. For instance, you can learn all about strings by typing "help (str)". As a result, you're going to get a significant amount of data on what strings are all about. That is why the "dir" and "help" functions are actually meant to go hand in hand. One uncovers the related methods and attributes, while the other gives you information about them. For instance, our above dir example told us that there's a function called "capitalize" related to the string class. The help function is going to tell us something along these lines:

capitalize (self, /) - Returns the capitalized version a string. It converts the first character of string to upper case and keeps the rest in lower case.

The "self" keyword means that any string we introduce to be capitalized is what's going to be capitalized. The forward slash is used to just signal the end of positional parameters. In other words, we can use parameters after it the same way we do when we define a function.

As you can see, we can have access to quite a great deal of information straight from the command prompt. However, for many people this isn't enough because the explanations are either quite basic or they use other terms that you're unfamiliar with. So, this function is best used with a bit of extra research, like using Python's online documentation files or simply Googling whatever you don't understand. There's no shame in it. In fact, being a programmer means you have to have serious research skills because a lot of your problem will be solved by looking for the solution others have already found. There's no need for each individual programmer to think how to reinvent the wheel.

Going back to our help function, at the end of each help page you'll have a "More..." option that you'll have to skip through. Instead, you can just use the Ctrl + C command to return to the prompt.

The help pages should be enough most of the time to learn what an attribute or a function does. However, the standard library documentation provided by Python developers is also a great resource if you want to get more technical. Just don't start memorizing everything or you'll go crazy. The reason all of these resources and options exist is so that you always have them at your fingertips instead of wasting your time learning them like poetry. Use all of these tools to learn as efficiently as possible.

Using Packages

One of the biggest reasons why Python is such a popular programming language is because it's modular. In other words, whether you're expanding into artificial intelligence, data science, machine learning, or game development, you don't have to reinvent things that already exist through various modules and libraries. Furthermore, everything can be divided into small components that you can shift around like Lego blocks. Actually, that is how a lot of projects are built, using the blocks (modules) created by other people in order to piece together an application. Someone has probably already thought about the functionality you need for your project, so all you need to do is find it, download it, import it, and use it.

Because Python is a modular language, you can simplify the development process whether you work alone or in a team. This is especially valuable if you work in a team because each member can work on a single component without waiting for each other to finish a certain part. Streamlining the development process greatly speeds up production, thus making Python the powerhouse it is today. The packages and modules that already exist help greatly because they have already been written and tested by other programmers.

You can find thousands of packages for Python, and one of the best places to find them is PyPi, which stands for Python Package Index. Head over to https://pypi.org/ and you'll discover too many packages to count. To install these packages, however, you'll also need a program. The most popular one is pip, which is a package manager that allows you to find, download, install, update, and delete any packages. In order to use pip, all you need to do is launch the command prompt and check if it's installed already. Many operating system versions already come with it pre-installed. Type the following command:

pip --version

If you don't have it installed, you'll need to download it and install it yourself, but that's an easy process just like any other application installation process. Once the manager is installed, you can check which packages are already installed:

pip list

Chances are you'll find quite a large amount of packages already installed. The list should be big, so you'll have to navigate through it to see all the packages. Another excellent source for packages is Anaconda's manager, which looks a bit better than pip. However, in this case you need to install Python with Anaconda, and you'll get a number of packages pre-installed along with the more efficient Navigator that comes with the program. Using the navigator, you can navigate to the "Environments" section and there you'll find a column containing a list with every single package installed. In addition, you'll also get a description telling you what the package is for.

Even though you can work with pip to install all your packages, if you want to use Anaconda to keep track of them and update them, you'll need to use conda instead because pip packages aren't immediately visible to Anaconda. So, just replace pip in any package commands with conda and you're good to go.

Alright, now that you have a quick startup guide to package managers and packages, we can start importing some modules.

Importing Modules

We already used Python modules quite a bit so you're familiar with the term, even though you may not fully understand it yet. The easiest way to grasp the idea of modules is to think about the Python standard library like a real library which has books (packages), and modules which are chapters in one of those books. Therefore, each package contains a collection of modules, while the library contains a collection of packages. However, it's the modules we're focusing on because they are what make Python a modular programming language.

So, in other words, we don't have to import an entire package, or all the modules it contains, in order to use a couple of chunks of code. Even when working with functions and classes related to dates and times, we can only import a part of them and not everything connected to them. However, it's perfectly acceptable to just import an entire module instead of just fragments of it. For instance, earlier when we worked with datetime we imported the entire module to have full access to everything that has something to do with dates and times.

While we only used one import method to gain data from modules, there are actually several ways to accomplish that. What we did so far was use the import command with the module we were interested in. So, when we needed higher mathematical functions, we imported the math module like so:

import math

After importing a module, we could also use the dir and help functions to find our way around. However, keep in mind that if you would use these functions on the module, like "dir(math)" you'd see an error. Why? The math package, like many other packages, isn't part of Python's standard library, so Python doesn't know about it unless you first install it. Once it's installed, then you can use the help function and you'll get all the details regarding the functions and methods contained within the math module.

Sometimes, however, we don't need the entire module, especially when we need to use several of them. There's no need to clutter your program if you can avoid it. So, in those situations, you can use the following syntax to specifically import what you need from the module:

from math import pi

This is probably the most common example. All we need is pi, so why import everything else inside the module? In the next example, we are going to make a reference to pi using math.pi. Take note that if you try to simply print pi you'll get an error:

print(pi)

NameError: name 'pi' is not defined

So right now, we don't have access to pi because it's not a component of the main library. We need the math module. So, we either import the entire module and then use the regular print function but attached to the module it belongs to:

import math

print(pi)

Not like this because this throws an error again, even though we have the module. We need to make a reference to it using the name of the module:

print (math.pi)

Take note that if you import only one component of the module, the dir and help function won't be available for that module, just the component. For instance, if we only use the pi element from the math module and try to use those functions, we'll get an error. Python knows only what we import. Don't forget that the dir and help functions are meant to be used to get a quick idea about what's going on. They're not something that will explain everything you need to know when developing a complex program.

In most situations, "from" is more efficient than "import" because you don't bring all the things you don't need to your development environment. In addition, you won't have to keep reminding yourself to use the name of the module before declaring its function. So, if you import just pi from the math module, you can refer to it as "pi" instead of "math.pi". This means that Python is now familiar with pi because it knows it's part of the math module, so you don't have to declare it as such.

Next, you might be wondering if you can import multiple components from the same module without repeating the line of code. The answer is 'yes'. You just need to seperate each element with a comma. Here's an example where we import the square root function together with pi:

from math import sqrt, pi

We can refer to both functions by their names without mentioning the math module. Here's how you can calculate the square root of pi using the two functions together:

print(sqrt(pi))

The result is:

1.7724538509055159

Finally, you can import modules using this syntax instead of the other two options:

from math import *

That asterisk tells Python to import everything inside the module. This is another way to say, "import math", however, there is one little detail that makes it different. Can you guess? When using the asterisk, all imported functions and methods are automatically associated with the module you downloaded. The command is actually more similar to those that specifically import certain components. In other words, you don't have to mention the name of the module to make a reference to a function. So, once you import everything you can simply type "print (sqrt)" and the function will work. However, while this seems like a handy way to download everything without having to constantly remind yourself to mention the module, most programmers don't appreciate the method. The reason is quite understandable, though. If you import too many modules this way, you're going to avoid using their names for reference so other programmers can end up getting lost in your code not knowing which function is part of which module. But, technically it's up to you because it works, nonetheless. Just try to avoid this method if you're working on a complex program with some teammates and you'll do just fine.

Build Your Own Modules!

While it may seem that modules are complicated collections of code, they actually aren't. They're pretty basic structures. Actually, each module is just a regular Python file like any of your code files and all they do is extend the code with more code. In other words, every time you write code for one of your programs and you save it as a file, you can say you created a module. Naturally, this doesn't mean you're using such files as modules because they might work as individual programs. Chances are the applications you've been developing so far are one file applications. However, if you actually want to build your very own Python module, you can do so. Why would you do that? Depending on your tasks and projects, you'll sometimes be able to take advantage of reusing some code you wrote earlier. So why not convert it into a module so that you can use all those functions, methods, and classes you already invested time and effort in? That's what this section is all about.

First of all, modules are Python files that end with the py extension and they have a regular filename like any other file. This means that the module contains Python code. So, let's say you have a number of functions that you've been regularly using to format dates, times or currency data:

1. myDate (myString): Pass a date into a string using the month, day, year format and then return a datetime date you can use in various operations or calculations.

2. dateString (someDate): This function will allow us to pass a Python datetime value and return a string that will contain a formatted date.

3. toCurrent (myNum, len): This function enables us to pass an integer or float type number and will return a string containing a dollar sign, decimal point commas, and two digits to represent the pennies. In addition, we have a "len", which is an optional value for the length. If we use it, the return value will have spaces on the left as a padding meant to match the length we specify.

import datetime

def myDate(myString):

Convert the date format string to a datetime.date value, or a None value

if the date is invalid.

try:

if len (myString) == 10:

myDate =datetime.datetime.strptime (myString,'%m/%d/%Y').date()

else:

myDate = datetime.datetime.strptime (any_str,'%m/%d/%y').date()

except (ValueError, TypeError):

myDate = None

return myDate

def dateString (myDate):

This will return a date string using the standard date format.

```python
# Pass either the Python date or the string date into that format.

if type(myDate) == str:

myDate = toDate (someDate)

# Check to see if we have a datetime that we're passing.

if isinstance (myDate, datetime.date):

x_date = f"{myDate:'%m/%d/%Y'}"

else:

x_date = "Not a valid date"

return x_date

def toCurrent (myNum, len=0):

# Now return the number in the form of a string with a dollar sign and comma
markers.

# Don't forget the length is optional.

x = "Not a valid amount"

try:

n = float(myNum)

except ValueError:

n = None

if isinstance (n, float):

x = '$' + f"{n:,.2f}"

if len > 0:

x = x.rjust(len)
```

```
return x
```

Feel free to create your own file with whatever functions you want. Take every chance to practice your own coding skills and don't just follow along. With that being said, if you run this code file, nothing will happen. It's not exactly a program that runs and calls these functions to do something. Instead, you need to take a series of steps.

In order to have access to these functions, you need to first add the file which contains them to the same location where your Python application's files are found. They all need to be in the same folder. Only then you can set up a new page and import the file in the form of a module. This process is done like with any other module import. Just type the keyword "import" followed by the name of the file (without the .py extension), like so:

```
import myfunctions
```

So even though the file is named 'myfunctions.py' you don't need to specify the extension. Don't forget you can also give the module a nickname if you want to make it easier to read in your code:

```
import myfunctions as mf
```

Now we have access to any of the functions we defined in our module. We just need to use "mf" as a prefix before naming the function in order to call it. Let's test them out and see if they work like functions from a standard library module:

```
# First, import all the code

# Since we're working with functions that involve dates,

# we also need to import the datetime module

# Then we introduce some basic testing information.

import myfunctions as mf

import datetime

today_date = "04.22.2020"

# This is a string date and we need to convert it to a datetime date
```

```
print (mf.myDate(today_date))

rightNow = datetime.today()

# This is going to display the date in a standard format.

print (mf.dateString(rightNow))

balance_dollars = 11111.222

# Use a currency format to display the balance.

print (mf.toCurrent (balance_dollars))
```

Now when you run the program, you're going to get an output. If everything goes well you should get a properly formatted date and the balance written in a standard format with a dollar sign, comma decimal separators and a separator for the pennies.

Remember that we discussed earlier that we don't have to use the module prefix if we import something specifically. That applies to custom modules such as the one we created as well. For instance, you can import just the "myDate" function if that's all you need, and in that case, you can skip writing the name of the module as the prefix to that function. Everything else stays the same as before.

Summary

In this chapter, we have summarized pretty much everything you need to know about Python libraries, packages, and modules. At least, it's enough to get you started in the right direction. This topic can cause some confusion because many inexperienced programmers want to stick to what they know, the core of Python. The three elements are often confused for one another as a result. So, remember that libraries are collections of packages, and a package is made of multiple modules. In turn, the modules contain a collection of functions, methods, classes, or even blocks of code that fulfill a specific task.

Modules extend the usability of the Python language. They are so important due to the flexibility they provide that they are one of the main reasons why Python is used as the main language in the fields of data science or machine learning. Python is modular, but the rules that you've learned so far regarding data types, functions, methods, and classes stay the same no matter what.

Chapter 7:

Python and the Internet

As a final chapter, we are going to explore Python's relationship with the World Wide Web and its ability to access the Internet programmatically. As you well know, the Internet has been integrated into every aspect of our lives. We are even making our homes smart through IoT devices such as smart locks, pollution monitors, and cybersecurity hubs. The Internet is everywhere, and someone needs to access it when developing software as well.

Programming languages like Python are capable of accessing any information on the web through the code you write. Accessing the Internet programmatically can open a lot of doors for you, so we're going to explore some basic aspects of Python's relationship with the web. You'll learn how you can access a website using Python, and you'll even explore the concept of web scraping used to gather massive amounts of data automatically.

Understanding the Internet with Python

The first thing that happens when you launch your favorite browser and click on a link is a request sent to the Internet, which then is redirected to a certain web server. This server then sends a response back to you. This response is what we refer to as a web page, however, it can be anything, for instance a file or a message. What's important to understand is that there are two components involved in this communication: you, together with the program used to communicate with the Internet, and the server that answers back to you.

This communication is performed through a URL, which is an address that tells the system what you're looking for. This stands for the Hypertext Transfer Protocol and that's why every web address starts with http or https. The difference between the two is the added security layer to the https addresses because it includes an encryption system instead of just sending unprotected data.

URLs can be simple or long and complex. They can contain the address for a folder, or a query string. They can also contain name and value pairs like those used in JSON data and dictionaries. However, when you're on the Internet, you only care about what you can see, namely the functionality presented to you in a neat package known as the user interface. Under all that there's a complex, messy world that involves two computer systems constantly talking to each other. This communication is done through what's known as HTTP headers.

You can't see the headers, but we can use various applications, like the web browser or Python to gain access to them. This is actually a useful feature because when you write code for web applications, you often need to see these headers. The easiest way to see them, however, is a program like "HTTP Headers" which is part of Google Chrome. Just navigate to the extensions menu of your browser to install it and then you'll see the header whenever you visit a website. We won't need all of the information made available to us. We just need the GET requests and the POST response. The information after GET is what the user requests and POST refers to data that we are transmitting to the server (for instance, when you post something on Facebook). Furthermore, we need what's in the second line after GET because that's where we see the status of the request. The first part of the status tells us which protocol is used, such as HTTP1.1. In this case it means the protocol follows the rules for version 1.1. Then there's a status code that tells us what's happening.

All of this information in this section is needed to access the Internet through Python. So, let's see what we can do programmatically.

Use Python to Open a URL

In order to gain access to the web from Python, we'll have to use the "urllib" package. This appropriately named library contains a number of modules that are used to access the Internet from a Python program. The most important module for us is the request module. This is the one that allows us to access data from the web. With that being said, this is the syntax we need to use when importing a certain module from a specific library:

from myLibrary import myModule

After importing the request module, we can open any webpage using the following syntax:

from urllib import request

myVariable = request.urlopen (url)

Take note that if you're not using a variable, then the URL has to be specified in between quotation marks. But if we store the URL in a variable, then we just call for the variable instead.

When we execute this code, we are going to get an HTTP Response object. With that being said, here's an example of how to access a simple HTML webpage, just so you get a better idea of the process:

```
from urllib import request

myURL = 'https://DominiqueSage.me/mysample.html'

# This isn't a real website, so you'll need to use another

# Now request the page you're interested in and store it inside a variable

myPage = request.urlopen(myURL)

# The response code we retrieve needs to be stored inside a variable.

responseStatus = myPage.code

# Confirm the data type of the page using the type function

print (type (myPage))

# Print the status code.

print (responseStatus)
```

The result will look like this:

```
<class 'http.client.HTTPResponse'> 200
```

This means that our variable holds an HTTP Response object, and that's all the server communicated to our request. The 200 at the end of the line is a status code that means everything works fine. You can find an entire list with those response codes to see what they mean, and you probably should, especially if you get a different code for some reason.

Web Scraping

When you receive a Webpage, it's transmitted to you in the form of HTML mixed with content. As you probably know, HTML isn't a programming language, but a markup language, and it is usually used with CSS to instruct your browser on how the content should be displayed. In order words, it's what controls the looks of the content you receive from a webpage. However, when you look at a page, it's not HTML and CSS that you see. You just see the actual content that is written inside HTML blocks of code.

In order to see the code that gives instructions to your browser, you need to press the F12 key. Do this on any webpage and a window will pop up showing you the source code of that page. Depending on the browser you're using, it might be another key, or you'll have to right click on the page and select Inspect or View Source. You'll see that the content is written in between body tags, like this <body> ... </body>. Everything is divided into sections, like the header, footer, ads, and so on. Another thing we're interested in is links, which are defined in between <a> </a> tags. These are known as anchor tags and they instruct the browser to transfer the user to a certain page based on the URL. Then we have <img> tags that define images, "src" attributes for the source of those images, and many more. If you want to learn more about HTML, check a brief tutorial online; it's a very simple language that you can learn in a couple of days.

This information is useful in combination with the tools offered by Python. By mastering Python programming and gaining an understanding about how the web works, you can start developing web-specific programs, or data gathering programs using web scraping. Web scraping is particularly useful in a world that always hungers for more data. This concept involves opening the page and breaking the data into segments that can be later analyzed. Python is perfect for such tasks.

To get started, we need to use two Python modules that are in fact part of Anaconda. If you already installed Anaconda, you just need to import them. Otherwise you'll have to download and install the additional software first. One of these modules is the request module part of the urllib. The purpose of this module is to enable us to send a request to the Internet to get a resource so that we can read it. The other module is known as BeautifulSoup (no, the name isn't made up). This module contains the tools we need to parse the page we retrieved and find the information we're interested in.

Now, to get started, create a new Python file and type the following lines to import the modules we need:

from urllib import request

from bs4 import BeautifulSoup

Now we need to let Python know the location of the web page we're interested in. Keep in mind that in order to scrap the page, it needs to be placed inside the code file. Preferably, we should also assign a variable to it, so we don't have to place the entire URL every time we need to call for it:

myPage = 'https://DominiqueSage.me/mysample.html'

Next, we need a new variable to get the page into the Python program. Then we can use the "urlopen" method to read it:

basepage = request.urlopen(myURL)

In order to parse the page, we'll need to copy the variable on a BeautifulSoup object that we'll just refer to as "soup". Take note that we also need to instruct the module that we want to parse this page. For that we'll need to specify "html5lib", like this:

soup = BeautifulSoup (basepage, 'html5lib')

As mentioned, most websites contain a lot of content code inside the various elements that make the page. However, the bulk of that content is normally in one single block. If you can learn which block that is, then you can parse the web code really fast. For the sake of the argument, let's say that content is placed between <article> tags. It often is, so it's usually a good guess. So, let's assign the content code to a variable and then parse only that section:

page_content = soup.article

Now that we isolated the content, we want to focus only on certain data, like URLs, image sources, and text. Since we want to collect this data, however, we need to store it somewhere. The easiest thing we can do is place it inside a list. So, let's create a basic list for that purpose:

myList = []

Next, we need to loop through the link tags inside the content. As mentioned, they all start with an <a> tag so they're easy to identify. In order to loop through them we can use the "find_all" method which is part of the BeautifulSoup module. Here's how it works:

for link in content.find_all('a'):

You'll now get a list of links with an image source, as well as text. We can separate these components by providing Python with the appropriate tags. Links use "a" tags, image sources use "src" tags, and text uses "span" tags. The next bit of code will filter these parts with the help of the get method, which is also part of the BeautifulSoup module. It will allow us to isolate each tag found inside the link, like so:

```
url = link.get ('href')
```

Now, let's obtain the image source and text source:

```
img = link.img.get('src')
```

```
text = link.span.text
```

Take note that for the text source we don't need the get method, because text isn't found inside HTML attributes like "href" or "src". Instead, it's in between span tags. Finally, we need to save the information we scraped so far before we can analyze another link. The easiest way to do it is using the append method to add the items to our list:

```
myList.append({'url' : url, 'img': img, 'text': text})
```

Done! Our data is stored during each loop cycle. There is a small chance that our scraping program might crash, because browsers are really good at going around certain HTML errors. So in case such errors exist, we should instruct Python to just skip the line of code that presents the issue. This is where you get to use try blocks once again. Here's how:

```
try: url = link.get('href')
```

```
img = link.img.get('src')
```

```
text = link.span.text
```

```
myList.append ({'url': url, 'img': img, 'text': text})
```

```
except AttributeError:
```

```
pass
```

Now we're ready to scrape some data!

Summary

Python is one of the most versatile programming languages out there, and this final chapter was meant to demonstrate that. If you go into web development or even data science, you'll want to have the knowledge to access the web programmatically and extract the data you need. This is just a taste of the possibilities, as there are many tools that Python and its wide array of modules provide. So, if you're interested in this aspect of Python programming, you already know enough to continue researching and advancing on your own.

Conclusion

Oh boy, what a journey. Going through all of these topics, one step at a time, reminds me of how exciting it is to learn a new language! Hopefully, some of that excitement has rubbed off on you, because contrary to what many believe, programming involves passion. It is indeed a science, but a good programmer knows how to spice it up with a dash of heart.

You may have finished adding another brick in the wall and have filled many gaps in your programming knowledge, however, you are far from done. Now you possess enough knowhow and experience to enter the real world. Start creating more and more complex projects. Look at popular programs and start figuring out how to clone them. Even by copying others you'll learn a great deal more. Be adventurous and be creative! Python is one of the very few programming ₤languages that allows you to do anything you can imagine.

Thank you for reading this book and learning how to master Python up to the expert level. The world always needs more programmers and developers. I hope you find that the book was helpful and that you have learned a great deal from it to Enjoy your coding!

References

Goldwasser, M. H., & Letscher, D. (2008). *Object-oriented programming in Python*. Upper Saddle River, NJ: Pearson, Prentice Hall.

Lutz, M. (2013). *Programming Python*. Beijing: OReilly.

Python 3.8.2 documentation. (n.d.). Retrieved from https://docs.python.org/3/

Zelle, J. M. (2017). *Python programming an introduction to computer science*. Portland, OR: Franklin, Beedle & Associates Inc.